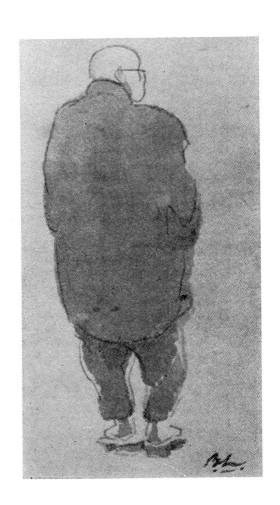

HAMADA
potter

Bernard Leach

 KODANSHA INTERNATIONAL LTD.

Tokyo, New York and San Francisco

Distributors

United States: Harper & Row, Publishers, Inc.
  10 East 53rd Street, New York, New York 10022

Canada: Fitzhenry & Whiteside, Limited
  150 Lesmill Road, Don Mills, Ontario M3B 2T6

United Kingdom: Phaidon Press Ltd.
  Littlegate House, St. Ebbe's Street, Oxford OX1 1SQ

Continental Europe: Boxerbooks, Inc.
  Limmatstrasse 111, 8031 Zurich

The Far East: Toppan Company (S) Pte. Ltd.
  Box 22 Jurong Town Post Office, Jurong, Singapore 22

Published by Kodansha International Ltd., 2-12-21 Otowa, Bun-kyo-ku, Tokyo 112 and Kodansha International/USA, Ltd., 10 East 53rd Street, New York, New York 10022 and 44 Montgomery Street, San Francisco, California 94104. Copyright © 1975 by Kodansha International Ltd. All rights reserved. Printed in Japan.

LCC 75-11394
ISBN 0-87011-252-x
JBC 1072-784629-2361

First edition, 1975
Second printing, 1978

To Mrs. Kazue Hamada,
who has supported and fulfilled
my friend's life.

5

CONTENTS

Preface

More often than not, a biography of one of the "greats" is of little actual value to those in the same profession who are working out their own problems a decade or more later. But I feel that Hamada in his thinking and approach to work sets an example and has a viable statement to make to craftsmen coping with today's problems. It is as well that my husband has not attempted a detailed historical biography of Hamada. Bernard has given his own evaluation and has chosen to let Hamada also make his own statement.

One rarely meets a person who, after spending several years studying and travelling, taking influences from many places, decided at the age of twenty-seven what he wanted his life style to be and proceeded in a straight, unwavering path to build this life. I believe that Hamada is the most completely integrated twentieth-century artist-potter we have; his home, his life-style, his thoughts and work flow in one harmonious stream.

To bring this book into being, Hamada and Bernard spent many hours almost daily for three months in a Tokyo hotel room discussing and reminiscing into a tape recorder. Our good friend, Mihoko Okamura did simultaneous translation in both languages. Both men are relatively fluent in the other's language, but the translation brought out subtleties of thought and nuances that otherwise would have slipped by. As I sat and listened to the rambling and chattering of these two verbose old men exchanging views matured over a lifetime, I learned a great deal. There is a deep friendship between them, and I found them both vivid and amusing to witness. It seemed that something was growing in this dialogue that was actually bigger than the sum of their observations and anecdotes.

We also selected articles by Hamada that we considered to have universal content and had them translated for Bernard to incorporate. I think it was vital that Bernard write this book, with and about Hamada. Nobody else could have done it. If Hamada were to write a book, his points of reference and his emphasis would be directed to the young of "New Japan". He spends much of his energy establishing folkcraft museums so that the heritage of Japanese folkcraft will not be lost to present and future generations.

The impact of meeting Hamada at Black Mountain College in the autumn of 1952 was so strong that it changed my entire life. I had previously left New York City for the country and spent two years by a brook, with the help of Bernard Leach's *A Potter's Book*, trying to find the mystery of the "good pot". I was feeling completely defeated and dissatisfied with my work when I walked into the Black Mountain studio and saw Hamada sitting high up, cross-legged in front of the wheel, throwing pots—someone else was below pushing the treadle for him. Suddenly I knew what was wrong—I was using the wheel like a lathe, tight and mechanically, while he sat there like a child playing with the clay. His hand movements were simple, and the clay was flowing, making the most free and organically shaped pots I had ever seen made on a potter's wheel. They were not always perfectly symmetrical, and as he took them off the wheel, he would pat them, maybe indent them—play with them. This experience started me in a chain of letters to Bernard Leach, who was on his way to Japan with Hamada and Yanagi.

Finally in the spring of 1954 I was allowed to go to Japan under Hamada's auspices for two years.

During this two-week conference at Black Mountain College, there were many "firsts". The Oriental pots were just coming out of the basements of American museums and being exhibited for the first time since the long Pacific war. A few Japanese craft exhibitions were also coming over. Many of us had been studying them and saying "If only we could get their fine quality brushes, our decoration would be better"—but when we asked Hamada about his brush that was gliding over the pots making beautiful sensitive patterns, he said it was from the scruff of a local dog in Mashiko! We then caught a stray, clipped pieces off his scruffy neck with nail scissors (and almost got bitten), bound the hairs together with sewing thread, tucked this tuft in a piece of hollow read, and had a better brush than we had ever owned.

Also several potter friends and I had been trying to get the effects of hakeme. We had tried worn-out paint brushes, old shaving brushes, etc., but nothing was right. One morning, while Hamada was decorating his pots, he stepped outside and collected some dry autumn grasses, tied them together with a bit of string . . . There it was—beautiful hakeme.

It was obvious how far away we were from the root of things in our preoccupation with tools, equipment, and technical know-how. So I went to Japan to see more of what Hamada represented.

This is an excerpt from an article I wrote about my first impressions of Mashiko in 1954.

> Mashiko, the El Dorado of many Western potters, is a small unpretentious village that has traditionally produced the kitchen ware for Tokyo. It came into existence with the establishment of Tokyo as the new capital, and potters travelled north from one of the best old potteries in Japan to found it on the remains of a pottery of a prior civilization.
>
> The mountains in this area are gentle and well wooded, and the valleys

are broad, making good rice fields. The potter and his wife and family raise their own rice and foodstuffs as well as carry on their work of potting. There is rarely a day when one does not see a swirl of smoke rising from some kiln being fired. It was in this simple remote community that Shōji Hamada chose to establish himself upon his return to Japan, after having worked with Bernard Leach when the St. Ives pottery was being established. He could have had a much higher position had he chosen to make his life in one of the cities, for he was a graduate of one of the best technical schools of Western ceramic science in Japan and had done extensive technical research before coming to England to work with Leach. But he wisely chose the more wholesome background of a traditional rural pottery and spent the first five years developing his own work whilst using the workshops of these potteries. Slowly and surely he grew, acquiring inner strength and assurance before he built his own kiln and workshop. Now his home is quite imposing. His houses, examples of the best old farmhouses of the area, are built of adobe-like stucco and huge wooden beams, with heavy thatched roofs two feet thick. His gardens are informal, and tucked inconspicuously along paths are outstanding examples of Korean sculpture. His love for the beauty of traditional buildings has led him to acquire them, and over all hangs the air of work as related to life, beauty coming from the daily way of things.

The day of my arrival at Hamada's was a memorable one. They were in the midst of glazing and stacking his large eight-chamber climbing kiln. Never had I seen so many pots being handled in so deft a manner. Hamada, his two sons, and about six workers were in a veritable forest of pots. The entire ground space under the huge kiln shed and the adjoining area outside and along a sloping path were thickly covered with boards full of pots. There were no clear pathways for walking anywhere; men with boards of pots over their shoulders were nimbly weaving over and around other workers as if in a long-rehearsed performance.

All glazing was done on the ground, either bending over large wash tubs pouring with a ladle, dipping, or squatting to decorate and to wash the bottoms of pots. Everyone seemed to know what to do and glided from job to job, anticipating each need and process beforehand.

Hamada does all the decoration on his own pots and more than half of it on stock items, in addition to indicating what is to be done to the others and instructing as to glazes and their treatment. I watched him decorate more than five hundred pots with wax and glazes in one day, sitting on a low stool with pots around him on the ground.

His best pots were reserved till late afternoon, for the more he worked the more vigour he had. The work was feeding him rather than draining him. His decorating techniques are principally glazes over glazes; sometimes over a thin yellow ochre slip, often with a wax pattern brushed on the first glaze; and his best-known technique is of trailing a large glaze pattern with a dipper. His brushwork is excellent, but he uses it only in large, sweeping patterns. About five thousand pots were in this firing, many quite large, and most of the glazing, decorating, and stacking was done in three working days. This number of pots represented less than two months' work (including bisque firing) by the two throwers (who have worked for him nearly fifteen years), his two sons, and himself. The kiln firing lasts two days, and the sight of men stoking small split sticks of pine into each chamber successively, with the resulting belching flames and smoke from the portholes, is highly dramatic. The temperature reached is about 1,250° C. No cones are used, temperature and heat dispersion being judged by eye.

To me his work cycle represented a miracle, without taking into consideration the quality of the ware. He prefers not to use mechanical equipment. The spirit surrounding the pottery is relaxed and free. Hamada has a hearty ease about him, which passes on to the crew and is reflected in the pots as well. There are few seconds, but there is also little apparent concern over the "imperfections of nature", and their thinking has not been influenced by our imposed standardization. Slick uniformity is not their conception of quality. In rural Japan there is no Sunday; work is continuous until firings. During the kiln watching, cooling, and opening there is a relaxed period of semi-holiday before preparations start for the next session of work.

I hardly made any pots at Mashiko because I was too overawed and involved watching how they did things. It was not the HOW of the "how-to-do-its"—there was a flow, a rhythm, an attunement to the material that I had not experienced before. I spent as much time watching an old carpenter as I did in the workshop.

Hamada is reluctant to talk "about pots", but he becomes ebullient when discussing the beauty in folkcraft—this is a concept he constantly expounds. When he received an invitation to go to Australia, he relates that they sent him a very fine schedule, which filled all his time with luncheons, meetings, and receptions honouring him. He said that he replied, "No, I will spend the week making one hundred pots, and we will fire them. The kiln opening will be the party, and I will distribute the pots to those involved."

We often see films or hear tales of traditional country potters from various countries who make a traditional ware they have made since childhood, which was made by their fathers, grandfathers, and possibly many generations before them. They are capable of using fantastic amounts of clay and producing an unbelievable quantity daily of pots of a prescribed shape. This type of information does us of this era no good whatsoever because we are not and could not be this type of potter. In this aspect Hamada is one of those who can help us translate. After I had been at Mashiko for six months, and had travelled with him and Bernard visiting several traditional pottery villages, he recommended that I go to work in one of these villages saying, "Don't learn what I learned, go and learn from where I learned it." I chose Tamba. The night before I left he told me not to concentrate on learning to make their standard ware. He said skill was cheap in Japan and I had not come for that. Every man in the village was more skilful than he. When he visited Tamba he said that I should be able to make about thirty medium-sized to large individual pots a day, every day. Many times I had left his own sitting-throwing room at night to go to bed and returned in the morning to see boards of yunomis—usually about seventy-five—by his wheel. When I said, "You must have worked very late last night", he replied, "No, only an hour." By working alongside the traditional potters most of his life, he has developed a capacity for spontaneity and rhythm in throwing, glazing, and decorating individual pots that we would all aspire to achieve. I often felt that I had been privileged to view the peak of Mt. Fuji, but could never climb the mountain to the top.

It is difficult to describe Hamada's throwing technique. For a large pot he beats a hole in the centre of the mound of clay with one hand as he pats the outside with the other. One or two passes brings it up, wavering, going blub blub, and you think he is going to lose it, but suddenly it pulls together and comes out even at the top. About the time you say to yourself, "Ah, I see what shape he is going to make", he has taken it off the wheel! It always amused me to watch potters with cameras and flash guns visiting him for the first time. They would crouch, poised, waiting for the final shot of the completed pot on the wheel, but it was completed in his eyes and taken off the wheel before they had snapped the shutter. Usually he made about three pots before they finally realized and snapped the shutter in time. He knows when to stop. I am sure that if anyone saw a board of Hamada's biscuited pots, they would discard them as too rough and unfirable, not realizing that he is leaving room for the thick ash glazes to play with the clay and for the fire to play with both.

Hamada's pots have become more colourful in the last few years; the blue of his salt glaze, an increased use of the rust-orange kaki, and also his exuberant use of red and green enamels from Okinawa. He has always loved the colour and vigour of these semi-tropical islands and latterly has spent his winters there. The colourful overglazed enamel pots he makes there will come as a surprise to those who have always emulated his quiet, "shibui" pieces.

On a recent visit, Hamada gave me a very free, loose pot made in Okinawa with extravagant red and green enamel decoration. A potter who was well acquainted with his work saw it and said, "Janet, I see you've acquired an early Hamada", but my answer was "No, it's his very latest." Sometimes it seems that an innocent boy has been turned loose with a paint box.

During the summer and autumn of 1954 I had watched him throw, decorate, and glaze and had seen all of the finished pots coming out of the kiln. Nevertheless, when I went to his annual exhibition in Tokyo in December I got a shock that I have never forgotten. There sat about seventy-five pots that I knew individually quite well, but a room full was something else. They just sat there like stones by the river-bed. They did not perform, they did not reach out and grab you, they were fulfilled within themselves and did not seem to care whether you liked them or not. These were his "shibui" pots. In the course of talking about himself for the book he told Bernard that he no longer felt he was climbing a mountain. Now he felt a sense of ease, as though he was strolling along.

As the three "greats" travelled across America from seminar to seminar in 1952, sometimes Hamada was misunderstood. It was his first visit to America; Yanagi was reading papers about the "Unknown Craftsman", and Bernard was lecturing about tradition, while Hamada gave wheel demonstrations. Some thought he was a peasant because he wore Japanese country clothes and chose not to speak English. Later, in Mashiko, while he was glazing he turned to me and chuckled, "When I was in America they thought I was a very simple person because I talked of ash glazes and they had long complicated formulas of calculated glazes. They did not realize that nature's glazes are infinitely more complicated than any man can conceive." Because of all the talk about tradition, many assumed he was a traditional country potter. They gradually realized that he was a very sophisticated artist with a superb eye who feeds on good crafts of all ages and all countries. He is constantly learning, looking, studying, even today, and he repeatedly goes to exhibitions and museums. Whenever he is in London, he not only goes to the museums he knows and loves so well, but he directs the taxi driver to the specific door he wants to enter, and he knows to which gallery on which floor he can go and see a certain pot.

I have accompanied Hamada many times through antique shops and markets of London. Seeing things through his eyes is an education. He buys large quantities of good articles for the new craft museum he is building at Mashiko. This gives him the excuse to buy the things he likes, but he is really buying them for himself—he wants to see them again. He calls it "eating them". His appetite is insatiable, and he collects avidly from every country and culture.

I have never referred to myself as a student of Hamada's. Instead I say that I have studied Hamada whenever and however I could over these twenty-odd years. While I was potting in Tamba, I always travelled to Mashiko for his glazing and kiln firings—telling him where I had visited, what I liked, and listening to advice. Often I found even one phrase from him so packed with content that it took me many nights of thought to try to understand the fuller meanings.

Janet Darnell Leach

Acknowledgements

Something rather remarkable occurred in the making of this book. It started with my English adaptation of Sōetsu Yanagi's essays, *The Unknown Craftsman*. A team was formed, drawn to these ideas and the men behind them. From Yanagi's aesthetics to Shōji Hamada's action, the distance is so short. This team, just getting to feel its own balance on the first project, entered into the work on this present book without breaking stride and perhaps with greater unity and rhythm. I think I speak for my companions when I say that it is the ideas themselves and their application that have provided nourishment in this effort.

To the members of this team—my wife, Janet; Mihoko Okamura; and Kim Schuefftan—thanks for everything you have done.

To Shōji Hamada, my gratitude for his sacrifice of precious working time and energy while making daily trips to Tokyo or staying in a Tokyo hotel to record on tape my interviews with him over a period of three months. Words do not and cannot fully convey thanks to this man, my friend, whose gift is the ability to give and who gives creatively.

To the Asahi Shimbun Publishing Company, for generously allowing us to use most of the color plates appearing here, my appreciation and thanks.

To Toyotarō Tanaka, Sonoe Asakawa, and the staff of the Nihon Mingei-kan, let me record the pleasure I have drawn from so many years of friendship and express my deepest thanks for generously providing permission to photograph my friend's pieces.

To Kodansha International, gratitude for lavish care and concern far beyond the usual practice, or economics, of the publishing trade.

I hope that our pleasure and excitement in making this book will be shared by all who read it.

Bernard Leach

St. Ives, Cornwall, 1975

15

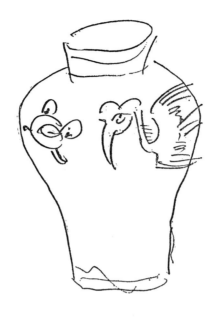

DIALOGUE

Dialogue

I have known Shōji Hamada for over fifty-five years. Our association in work and friendship has been a very special one. Shōji Hamada came to me as a young man and asked to come to England with me; we came to St. Ives together fifty years ago and set up a pottery where there had been none, building the kiln, the workrooms, the house—much of it with our own hands—then digging the clays, chopping the wood to fuel the kiln, making pots and experimenting, and finally exhibiting in London and Tokyo. But also after Hamada's return to Japan in 1923, the strands of our lives continued their interplay in all sorts of ways, mostly working ways in pottery and the crafts movements, criss-crossing, interweaving, and running smoothly together repeatedly. Now, in 1973, we are together going over our record of the past and we are still interchanging ideas on present issues and work in hand. It is in this way I have constructed this working portrait of Shōji Hamada, a portrait to which he has contributed in his direct and lively way, completing the story that in so many ways is the story of both our lives. These pages show how this web of common interest—the pursuit of standards, the making of good pottery—has unrolled from 1919 to the present day.

I have wondered which would be the best way to approach the man and his character. I think the simplest is to start at the beginning. That was sometime early in 1919, when I was living with Sōetsu Yanagi (the founder of the Japanese folkcraft movement) at Abiko, a village some twenty-five miles north-east of Tokyo, by the banks of a lagoon that stretched away six miles towards the rising sun. One day a letter arrived, in rather clear and bold handwriting, which impressed me by its look and still more by its content; it also impressed Yanagi. It told of a young man, about twenty-four, who as a lad had intended to become an artist. But he had changed his mind and decided to take up pottery as his profession, and after graduation from a technical college he took employment with the Ceramic Testing Institute in Kyoto.

From there he wrote, asking whether he could come up and meet me at Abiko and whether it would suit my old friend Yanagi. We both said yes, we want to see this man. He came some days later, and the first moment I saw him, I think

I felt that here was somebody whom I would like. I soon learned that he had studied all that side of the approach to potting that I had not—the technical side, the chemical side; he had gone to a school founded for that purpose. But he had not been trained as a hand potter—he wanted to pursue this, and when we met and talked more deeply, he said that he had had enough of the scientific approach to potting, he wanted the approach of the hands, and of the heart behind the hands.

Hamada:

As a boy I wanted to be a painter, not a potter. During the third year of junior high school, I concluded that I should either become a master painter or the whole idea was meaningless. I felt that it was necessary to be better than the best. My reasoning went something like this: the traditional Japanese description of Mt. Fuji likens it to a pure white fan upside-down. People thought of Mt. Fuji in this way. But then came Taikan Yokoyama, who painted a misty, vague, not so beautiful Mt. Fuji with a round instead of a painted peak. The public's image of Mt. Fuji changed with this artist. After him came Ryūzaburō Umehara, with his paintings of a red, bumpy, rocky, ugly Fuji, and the young people began to say that this was the true Fuji. Thus, the standards of beauty in Japan changed according to the artist's eye. This is one reason I wanted to become an artist.

My father had wanted to be a painter too and had begun to learn painting at the age of fourteen. He used to show me his work when I was a child, which is certainly another reason for my ambition.

It was this aim that impelled me to visit galleries on my way home from school. At that time, over sixty years ago, at the back of the Mikasa Gallery in Ginza was a painting by Ryūsei Kishida of a man with bushy hair, metal-rimmed glasses, and sharp eyes. It was a portrait of Bernard Leach. Displayed also were pots and etchings by Leach and pots by Kenkichi Tomimoto. This was my first encounter with Leach's work. Whenever I went there on my way home from junior high school, I looked forward to seeing some change in the display, but Leach's, Tomimoto's, and Kishida's works never seemed to sell; they were always dusty. The occasional changes were a pleasure because it meant there would be something new for me to see and enjoy.

I remember being captivated by a small pitcher made by Leach. I had seen it and admired it on every visit to the Mikasa Gallery, but could not afford it. Curiously enough, I am now the owner of it, for many years later it was given to me by a friend, who found it in a Kamakura antique shop. I had also wished to own some of Tomimoto's pieces, but they were also too expensive for me.

At about this time I had another opportunity to see some of Leach's work. On Rodin's seventieth birthday the Shirakaba group of Japan sent him some *ukiyo-e* woodblock prints, and Rodin was so pleased that he in return sent three sculptures—two heads and a standing figure. The group took the occasion of this gift to hold an exhibition at a place called Sankaidō, and Leach's works were displayed there along with Rodin's.

Besides going to galleries, art books were an important source of inspiration. In a book about the Post-Impressionists, I came across the statement by Renoir, which said something like: "If half the would-be painters in France were transformed into craftsmen, it would benefit both painting and the crafts: the number of painters would be decreased, and the decorative arts would get able people." This statement gave me courage to change my whole aim. It summarized my own thinking, and the fact that my ideas were endorsed by a great painter made a deep impression. Why not be a potter? Pots can be used, they have a function. Even a bad pot has some use, but with a bad painting, there is nothing you can do with it except throw it away.

I did not know where to go to learn pottery in Tokyo. The name of the potter Hazan Itaya was familiar to me, and I had heard that he was teaching at the Tokyo Industrial College—which was the only school in Tokyo that taught ceramics. I decided to enrol there.

Itaya was an excellent teacher. He said he never took apprentices, but that I could visit him at home when I desired. I used to go on Sundays and gradually I came to know the story of his difficult life. Once, when I looked up, I noticed a tea-pot on the shelf in his room. It resembled the ones used in my early school years, so I asked him where it was made. He replied that it was not too far from his home town, at a place called Mashiko, a country town north of Tokyo. It was this tea-pot that brought me to Mashiko in later years.

The work of Leach and Tomimoto had shown me the direction I wanted to follow. The apprentice system was a thing of the past; there was no appropriate master, so I had to learn pottery techniques in a school. There one had to learn the scientific aspects—chemistry, etc. The most difficult subject for me was calculus, but it was required. A school is always a school, and I spent the first two years solely on laboratory work. It was only in the third year that we were given a certain amount of freedom to do what we wanted.

The potter's wheel course lasted only two weeks. The students used the wheel in turn, and the least interested ones were able to complete the course without even touching the wheel. I was not satisfied with the short drill courses and started to hand model. On the other side of Tokyo there was a ceramic workshop where they sold clay and fired pieces for you. I used to go there every Sunday. Later, I found out that Kanjirō Kawai was also a regular visitor there.

It was Kawai who first sought me out. After introducing ourselves, he blurted, "You want to be an artist-potter do you?" I replied in the affirmative. Kawai said, "So do I. Do you know that there are thousands of students who graduate from this school, but only you and I have this ambition?" This thought, of course, excited us both.

Kawai graduated the year after I entered the school, so we had known each other less than a year when Kawai said that he was going on to work at what was called the Kyoto Ceramic Testing Institute. I think it had been run by the city, but it was just being converted into a government-run institution, which meant the salary would be very small.

Once he was settled in Kyoto, Kawai invited me to visit him. A year before

21

graduating, I made a journey to see for myself the pottery centres I had read about and studied. I went to Tajimi in Gifu Prefecture, to Nagoya to visit Seto and Tokoname, then on to Yokkaichi, Shigaraki, and finally to Kyoto.

In Kyoto I went to see what Kawai was up to and how he was faring at the institute. Poor Kawai was still in his old student's uniform because no salaried position had opened yet, nor was he at a stage where he was able to learn anything. His job was testing glazes with a Baumé hydrometer: "I didn't study enough at school, so I didn't know how to use the hydrometer. My boss got angry, and I thought many times of leaving," said Kawai with a laugh. Watching Kawai, I decided to come to this Kyoto Testing Institute after graduating even if there was no position open. Kawai said he would be waiting for me.

On the way back from Kyoto, I felt that I would like to see something more, so I went to the Kutani pottery area near Kanazawa and again to Nagoya, Tokoname, and Shigaraki.

When I finally graduated, I went on to the institute where Kawai was. Fortunately, someone left the institute just then, so I got that position, which paid thirty yen a month. The pay was enough for a bachelor like me. I could not spend more than five yen on food a month no matter how extravagantly I ate.

Visiting Buddhist temples in Kyoto was our daily nourishment. Also each Sunday we went to nearby Nara to visit Tomimoto, to watch him work and see how he was getting on. We looked forward to these weekend trips. We got off at Koriyama, a small village, and pushed a little railway handcar to Tomimoto's house. It was in the middle of a rice field, the kind of scene you come across in Tomimoto's paintings and drawings. There was no gateway; we saw his chimney and kiln immediately. What struck us as strange was a pile of empty tin cans. I had heard that Tomimoto had been abroad and knew London, Paris, etc. My first impression was of this pile of tin cans. I smelled an air of sophistication before meeting the man, and knew at once he must be eating very luxuriously because of this selection of exotic tin cans outside his kiln. Once we had met, I found him to be a man of elegant tastes. At the same time, when we discussed work, I could see that he was very advanced for a Japanese artist. His way of thinking and his talk were extremely interesting and opened many windows for me.

I realized then that the two "grand champions" of pottery were Leach and Tomimoto. There were no others, I felt, who equalled these two, and I knew that there was no better time to start my own potting. I said to myself that the only thing to do was to work hard with Kawai and not to worry about anything else.

I remember well that at Tomimoto's home I had a lunch in which he served *kimpira gobo*, burdock root shavings, sautéed in sesame seed oil and spiced with red pepper. Tomimoto asked me whether I liked this dish, and I said, "Very much". But what impressed me was the fact that the meal was a mixture of Eastern and Western style cooking. Later I felt this even more strongly, when I met Yanagi and experienced his eating habits. This experience with Tomimoto must have been around 1916, because I spent four years at the institute before going to England with Leach.

Though I was in Kyoto, I wanted very much to see any exhibitions by Leach,

Tomimoto, Ryūsei Kishida's Sōdōsha group, and the others. Whenever the opportunity came, I would go to Tokyo on the Saturday night train. The train then cost ¥2.80, so even with a very small salary one could afford to go to Tokyo in those days. I would spend the whole Sunday in Tokyo and return that night, again on the night train. Then I would go and give a full report to my good friend Kawai.

The most costly things were books. Especially, the bill I received from Maruzen bookstore for imported books occasionally exceeded my monthly pay. On pay days I was invariably visited by a person from Maruzen, who collected twenty yen every month. This young man stayed with Maruzen. Many, many years later we would meet, and he would say that he always felt sorry for me when he had to collect the money.

Today, Japanese books on ceramics are countless, but at that time our printing methods were poor, and most of the books with illustrations were imported, expensive ones. Every time I glanced through Maruzen's monthly book catalogue I heaved a deep sigh.

The most talked-about publication at that time was an expensive pair of books on Chinese ceramics written by R. L. Hobson. Fortunately, Kawai had a sponsor who had a library, and we were given access to books too expensive for the institute or us to purchase.

We came across one book that truly captivated us. It was a book—a pictorial record—of an exhibition at the Metropolitan Museum in New York. It was cheap and thin, with only black-and-white illustrations but it introduced a number of Chinese and Korean ceramics. The book helped us a lot in our studies, and I still can remember the pictures from the first page. Kawai said, "I'll make this!" and I said, "I'll make that!" and later we compared our experiments with Sung dynasty glazes.

Kawai was especially carried away with trying to produce copper-red glazes. He was enchanted by the copper-red effects on jars and bowls of both the Sung and Yüan dynasties. However, we did not understand the true colour and quality of these glazes. After all, we saw neither the real thing nor the actual colour. All we did was read the explanations and repeat our tests.

Then someone told us that Mr. Shinsuke Hayashi, a fine art dealer in Kyoto, had some genuine Chinese pieces. We visited Hayashi, scrutinized the real thing, and finally understood the methods. For about a year thereafter we were obsessed with copper-red glaze. Kawai never lost his love for this colour. Even before he learned the correct techniques, I remember that he painted an unglazed jar in red and left it by his pillow before going to sleep. For nearly fifty years Kawai never allowed even a single kiln to be fired without some copper red. Of all ceramic artists, I believe none ever surpassed Kawai in the pursuit of this glaze.

Leach seems only to have exhibited in Tokyo, whereas Tomimoto exhibited in places like Kyoto as well. But whenever Leach had a show, I went to see it and I feel that I saw most of them. He exhibited in Ginza and thereafter at a gallery called Ruisseau in Kanda. At the Ruisseau exhibition, not only were there pots made by Leach but there was furniture that he designed—a sofa and chair. The chair was upholstered with material that was inspired by the stitched and quilted Japanese firemen's coats and was designed so the material could be stretched taut when it sagged by pulling it through the frame of the chair. This was very interesting for me to see. There were also a small rug with a fine pomegranate pattern, block-printed textile hangings, and heads for women's hat pins in raku pottery and in porcelain. All of these things were very close to life, to living, and very exotic and unusual.

Even then, when I was working in the testing institute with a salary, I could not afford a drawing by Leach. Kawai wanted one too and asked me to try to get him one if I could. I remember a particular one of a girl at a shrine playing a flute, but what was most interesting for me was that, even if Leach's drawings did not sell at a particular exhibition, he had the gall to exhibit them again at the next exhibition. Usually, in Japan, if something did not sell in one exhibition it never made an appearance again. But in Leach's case, if his drawings did not sell, it seemed that it was not the fault of Leach but of the viewers, so he tried again. Sometimes, even ten years later, a particular piece would make another appearance. It impressed me very much because it was his own work, that is to say, he knew that he was one hundred percent in it—it was *his* work, he believed in it, and he felt free to exhibit it again. In most cases an artist tries to be fashionable or to imitate something, so that the artist himself tires of his own work of a particular period and does not want to look at it again after, say, three years. Such artists are not true to themselves, and their work is short-lived. In the case of Leach's work, it did not have to have a time or a period—it did not even have to sell. We Japanese were very impressed with this aspect of Leach, this British stability, the solidness of tradition, not being whipped around by fashion. Leach is beyond time; therefore, even in his 1973 exhibition there were many early pieces—and how interesting they all are to look at.

Much later, I got a real surprise when I was trying to find frames for some drawings Leach sent to Japan. Some of the drawings were done on the cheapest Japanese toilet paper, which I had taken to England. The paper was full of holes. I well know the Western seat toilets, and the suspicion was unavoidable as to where Leach did those drawings. His early paintings were very funny and interesting in that respect.

Tomimoto used to say, "Don't ask Japanese potters about potting because they won't tell you the truth." Yet Kawai and I, Leach and Tomimoto were like two pairs of hungry sparrows—whenever we found good "food", we exchanged information, saying where we found the food, how we found it, what the food was. Leach often tells the story of how he and Tomimoto exchanged correspondence and of the time when postcards crossed and arrived the same day, each giving the other identical information about his own findings. This kind of coincidence shows their growth was advancing at a very similar pace, and the attunement, the closeness they had together in working spirit.

Hitherto I had only observed from a distance. I did not attempt making conversation with Bernard Leach at that time; perhaps about 1918 was the first time that we spoke to each other, but only very briefly at some exhibition. It was only in 1919 that a real exchange took place. Leach invited me to come to Abiko to see his workshop and also to see what he was doing with his glazes. He wanted my criticism and opinions about how things were working. The best place to do it was at his workshop, so that is how I got to see his place in Abiko.

Leach:

I think Hamada stayed for three days, I cannot remember exactly, but those three days, barring sleep and food, were fully occupied with interchange and many comments and questions from Yanagi himself. Here was somebody who was obviously sensitive, who had a broad and easy flowing sort of mind. He had been doing a lot of meticulous experimental work; I think he said as many as ten thousand tests in imitation of Chinese glazes. Here was someone who could tell me why such and such a thing happened—what reduction firing was, for example. I had not met anyone yet with whom I could fully communicate as a potter, and here was a Japanese who spoke enough English, which, combined with my Japanese such as it was, enabled us to converse freely.

Hamada:

I remember arriving at Abiko station and seeing a man and his wife alight from another train coach. There were only two cars waiting at the station. The couple took the first car. I immediately recognized them as Sōetsu Yanagi and his wife. For one thing, he was carrying a coarse woven bag from Taiwan. By coincidence, I had just got an identical one myself at a shop in Tokyo where they sold Taiwanese articles and had it with me. He rode off with his wife, so I knew immediately in which direction to walk because I knew Leach worked at Yanagi's home. I followed and arrived somewhat later, just before noon. I was shown into the house and was waiting for Leach to appear when suddenly the door burst open. In came Naoya Shiga calling out for Yanagi, "Are you there, Yanagi?" He was taken aback to see an unknown face in the room. He begged my pardon and then asked me what I was doing there. I replied that I was waiting for Leach, that I was a young potter, and so forth.

"Are you a potter? Then I have a question to ask you that I have been rather concerned about for some time." Shiga had inherited a number of tea-bowls and things from his father and did not quite know what to do with them, Should he sell them or not? There happened to be one very good Karatsu teabowl with a cross mark at the foot. The curio dealer wanted to give a very small price for it, and Shiga was not sure whether he should let it go for that price or not. He wanted my opinion. He asked about the Karatsu glaze, what kind of brush was used to make the decoration, and so forth. I explained that the decoration of the teabowl was not of pigment as is usually the case, but that black glaze was used somewhat like the hakeme method. Shiga responded, "Well then, I must take good care of it and value it if this is true." Then he went on to ask about a type of blue-and-white ware—what were its good points, whether the good pieces were in Japan or in China, and the like.

We were still conversing when Yanagi came in and invited us to join him in the next room. Upon entering, I saw two scrolls hanging in the *tokonoma* alcove, each with a large Sanskrit character; in the middle of the alcove was a Po-shan incense burner, and on one side was a large jar. There were no Korean articles yet. Perhaps he had some, but at any rate I did not see anything Korean in his room. What impressed me very deeply was the uniqueness of the decor. It was so refreshing to see the unconventional way in which the whole room was done; every impression was new to me.

The next room was the dining room, where all kinds of food were served in all kinds of ware. This was all the more startling for me because the food on the table and the manner in which it was being consumed was even more unique than the experience with Tomimoto. I had brought with me a special preserved black bean (*Daitoku-ji nattō*) from Kyoto as a gift, and it made an appearance on the table in one of Leach's dishes.

Leach began with bread first, while the Japanese were having their rice first and bread later. It was wonderful to watch everybody adjusting freely to his own life-style. This was the life-style that Tomimoto and Leach had chosen, and I felt that it was the truest way to live out this particular period, this time of history, and how fitting it was for me also to join in such a way of life. This was true life, I felt. I ate a little of what was served me and even joined in eating the *nattō*—what Leach called bean cheese—spread on bread! This, too, was not only good, but a most interesting way of combining foods. I thought it very unique.

It seemed that Leach was preparing for an exhibition, and therefore his studio was full of furniture and pots and things. One chair made of Japanese cedar impressed me. There were very few straight lines; soft curves were used, marvellous forms, marvellous lines—I saw the same feeling for line throughout his work.

Technically, I had a lot to say about pottery, but on the whole it was I who had much to learn from this group of people.

Leach:

I think I'd better break in about the chair he speaks of, a three-legged chair from my little workroom. I became tired of sitting on the floor and wanted support for my long legs and so forth, a little more comfort and a rest for my back. So I got hold of the carpenter and said, "I would like to find, if possible, some local wood with the natural curve of the grain like the kind used in roofs of houses and Buddhist temples. I've drawn the curve of my own back as a guide." "Oh," he said, "Yes, I'll take you along and see what they've got." He did, and I found a naturally bent piece of Japanese cedar. It was just the right curve; the wood was about three feet in diameter and it was possible to cut parallel with the curve and make quite a number of chairs with that back. And that's what I got him to do. He put on the three legs, thrusting them into the seat as we do with dinner chairs. This light wood made a chair that I still have in my room in St. Ives.

At the end of each day the workmen made a bonfire of the straw mats used to wrap charcoal, which were very dry and burned very quickly. The workmen would gather round the burning straw to warm themselves on cold evenings before going home. There I toasted the whole chair, as I was told to do, so that it was seared all over. Afterwards I rubbed it with a wet cloth until it got a polish that is still there—it has lasted almost sixty years.

Hamada:

How good it was that I came to Abiko. Rather than discuss ceramic chemistry and glazes, just seeing the objects before me and around me was an experience that has never been forgotten. The studio itself was Chinese in style, almost as if it had been brought over intact from China. It had a circular doorway. No Japanese could ever have thought of this. Only Leach would have thought of making such a studio. How refreshing it all was.

There were many drawings; some were decorations that Leach used for his pots, and others were simple sketches. I remember there were some pigeons with peculiar tails. Then there were two birds inverted, and swallows—I remember being extremely impressed with the swallows. Then, of course, Leach's "Temple of Heaven" was there, and "Hakone". I remember the stove in the room very well. I think the "Chelsea Church" was also there, but despite the fact that it was characteristically Western in feeling, I do not remember being very impressed with it. I much preferred Leach's "Hakone" and the more scenic drawings that he did once he came to the East.

There was also an etching called "Lagoon", which I thought was very fine. Later, in St. Ives, when Leach wanted to make more prints of it, I was asked to polish the plate. I remember polishing it too well, and Leach was very troubled because it was too clean. I had done too good a job on it.

Leach:

With regard to that "Lagoon" etching, it was of that lagoon by the margin of which Yanagi's house stood. The time was dusk. We had been out in a punt and coming back we had seen a fisherman, a man who fished there for a living, lean over the very edge of his punt with a basket in his hand, pressing down amongst the reeds and trapping a fish. I was impressed by the movement first of all, the rising up of the bow of the punt with the weight of the man at the other end, the fact that he was catching a fish in such a simple manner, and carried the image in my mind to Yanagi's house and there drew it in pencil. The next day, I think, I got my zinc plate ready with the preparation for a soft ground etching. So the whole memory—the time, the lagoon, Abiko itself, my friends—was a way compressed into the mood; I think something of that sort must have been transferred onto the plate.

Hamada:

I received a great deal from that first visit to Abiko, but I did not have any time to leave anything in return. I was so busy being impressed, so busy looking and absorbing. Then not so long after that was the fire at Abiko.

Leach:

Hamada seems to say he left nothing behind. With this I cannot agree. Always there was, I think, a give and take. He went back to Kyoto to his testing institute. By that time, I believe, he was doing a good deal of the work in the production of what are called Seger cones for measuring temperatures in kilns. I think I remember him correctly saying that he was looking forward to the time when he could put theory aside in favour of practice, and that he had reached the point at which he could trust the senses with which he was born in estimating how much material was required for a particular purpose. He was not a man given to casual statements.

The next time I saw Hamada was when I went to Kyoto and visited him and Kanjirō Kawai, his friend. I saw some of Hamada's pots—I remember going to his own workroom; it was not in the testing institute but in some street where he had a big room in which he could make pots on a wheel. The young man had bought a wheel with his own money to practise on in his own time. He pointed out one large pot, with a slightly wry smile, saying he had made it too big to get out of the room, but not intentionally. I thought it was odd that he should, with his amount of practical experience, make a pot too big to get out of the room. It seemed astounding, but it was certainly evidence of great enthusiasm. He had not made many pots of his own and he wished to get to that point where he could begin to express his ideas and to become a potter.

Backing and advising him were three old men, three comrades, who had retired from their main activities in life. These men were appointed by fate, as it were, to be this young man's mentors. One, Sōzan Iseki, had been a follower of Zen and had been living for a time in a Zen monastery. I met him several times—quite a remarkable man. He later became a lawyer (curious mixture!). Of him, I think, Hamada was almost afraid. At any rate, Hamada gave much weight to what this man said, whose words were sharp like those of a Zen master. Besides Iseki, there was Hamada's father, who had retired from business. He had had a factory for making ink, on the banks of the Sumida River in Tokyo. Then there was Mr. Okada, who was the proprietor of the Heiandō, the firm making the best calligraphy and artists' brushes in Tokyo. But to these three I will return presently. Meanwhile I think I should say something about what I was doing in Abiko.

I had been there about a year then, after my return from a year in Peking. I found amongst Yanagi's books one published in England quite some time before by a man called Lomax, entitled *Quaint Old English Pottery*. I do not like the word "quaint", but it was the only book that really told about Toft ware and was well illustrated. This was my first attempt after having started making pots in an alien country to get my feet on the ground of English tradition.

It was not very long after Hamada first came up from Kyoto to meet us that a terrible thing happened—a very bitter experience, which was nevertheless a good thing in the long run. I learned the power of flame. While firing the stoneware kiln in preparation for an exhibition in Tokyo, my kiln shed caught fire during the night, and the whole thing burned to the ground. When I was called early in the morning, the brick kiln stood there alone, stark. I wondered what I could do during the year before I was to return to England without a workshop and money to live on and pay for the journey home. Help came to me in an amazing way. Friends whom I had helped brought me old recipes and new ones as well and I was able to use the kiln rebuilt on Viscount Seiki Kuroda's land in Tokyo, near my house, with the assistance of one experienced potter and a boy to do odd jobs, owing to his incredible generosity. Work went ahead very smoothly and the relationship with the two assistants was marvellous. During this last year before my return to England I was in constant touch with Hamada, asking him technical questions (especially chemical) about which no one until then had been able to inform me, and getting helpful answers. Hamada was also instrumental in advising me about sources of materials.

9/26 [1919]

Mr. Leach,

Yesterday your letter arrived. That your move to the new house in Komazawa must have been trying, I also can very well understand. I think it is a shame that you searched for my letter for one hour when you had so many things to do. You are so busy, I always think it is an imposition to write these letters in this difficult-to-read romanized Japanese.

I have recopied the reply to Mr. Naka and think it should already have been delivered to you.

A.   The *gosu* [impure cobalt] test will be sent after we try to fire it here.

B.   I understand. I did not realize it was lead [in reference to a previous inquiry]. In Kyoto there are the following two hand wheels.

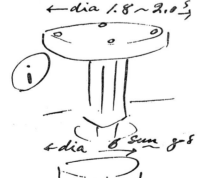

Revolved with an accessory "turning stick".

This is also called a "small [banding] wheel". It can be carried anywhere and is used when lines are to be drawn, etc.

Am I wrong in presuming that, having bought the (i) wheel, you also need a (ii) wheel with a 1-*shaku* diameter? Don't you need both now?

C.   The shop that sells materials is

Tamiya Shokai

Aioi-cho 1 chome, 5 banchi

Honjo-ku

Materials not available there I will send from Kyoto, so please reply.

D.   I will comply with your request regarding *kote* [wooden profiles], *hera* [wooden or bamboo blades], and *shira-e* [white slip].

E.   Should I send these things to Mr. Kuroda of Azabu? Today I received ¥50 from Mr. Naka.

When the day I go to Tokyo is decided, I will inform you immediately. Though I by all means wish to go in October, since the testing institute workshop will be busy for some time, I do not know when the trip will be possible.

Since I was born near Tamagawa, I know Komazawa well.

Recently I met Mr. Tomimoto twice. He wished to send a book of "recipes", but was worrying if the Komazawa address was correct. When I send the samples etc., I will also send the "recipes".

S. Hamada.

I will send a little *ōdo* [ochre].

10/19 [1919]

Mr. Bernard Leach,

Yesterday I sent the goods you requested to Mr. Naka. I am sending a list with this letter, so please check. There are three parcels, containing Seger cones, *isubai* [*isu* wood ash; high calcium content], and other things. The *isubai* parcel will probably arrive a little later than the others.

I was thinking only of the materials and I completely forgot to send the *kote* and *hera*. Please forgive me. I will send them with the *gosu* [impure cobalt] test within 2–3 days. I definitely want to send the *gosu* test in time for your first experimental kiln on the 23rd.

Here are the replies to your questions.

Benigara [red iron oxide]:

This can be made by recalcining red earth with a large Fe content, then washing it in water, but a good product is obtained by calcining (400°–700° C.) *rōha*, "green vitriol".

Hana konjo (smalt):

This is cobalt glass powder. Add 0.5–1.5% cobalt oxide (by

weight) to *shiratama* (lead silicate) and grind well. If it is strong, add a little *tō-no-tsuchi* (lead carbonate).

 Shiratama or *tama* (glass or frit):

There are many varieties. The *shiratama* for overglaze enamel is the most difficult. Depending on the pottery, special materials are added and the process is kept secret, but, generally, it can be made with the following materials.

keiseki (or *hinooka*)	[quartz]	12
tō-no-tsuchi		26
		(by weight)

Heat these strongly in a crucible until they melt and form glass, then pour into water so it will shatter into a fine powder.

 Flux:

To the *tama* just produced, add

tama	25		20
tō-no-tsuchi	20	or	11
keiseki	4.5		1.3
	(by weight)		

and grind well. If you add metal oxides to this flux, various overglaze colored enamels can be made.

([*in Leach's hand*]	
Shiratama flux	50
w. lead	40
quartz	8
copper carb.	3)

Aodama [green enamel]:

flux	100
$CuCO_3$ (or *rokusho*)	2 (or 3)

Murasaki dama [purple enamel]:

flux	100
gosu (or manganese oxide)	0.5–1

bright purple

stoneware red glaze	5–10

Kidama [yellow enamel]:

flux	100
benigara [red iron oxide]	3 (quiet)
or	
lead carbonate	2 (bright)
or	
tō-jirome [antimony oxide]	3 (a little quiet)

If the *kidama* that was sent is too pretty, you may add a little *benigara* or *tō-jirome*. I will send the *tō-jirome* together with the *gosu* test.

If the flux is weak, add *keiseki*; if strong, add *tō-no-tsuchi*.

 Kurogosu:

This is manganese peroxide (MnO_2). I think it is best to use natural cobalt (*kyūgosu*) or *kyūgosu* mixed with *kurogosu* for the drawing of the "black line" under overglaze enamel.

Rokusho:
This can be made by leaving copper in a damp place for a long time, but to produce it in quantity, place the copper in acetic acid. But this takes a rather long time and is tedious.

Aka (red enamel):
There is no quiet red. If you add a little *benigara*, it will become quiet. If it gets too strong, add a little *tama*. The *benigara* is extremely good, so I sent you 50 *momme*.

Ōdo [yellow ochre]:
As it is or mixed with another clay to lighten the colour, you can use this with raku (becomes reddish) or with stoneware (brownish black) slip. With raku, if it does not stick well, add a little *tō-no-tsuchi*.

Irabo glaze: (S.K. 8)	*dobai* [wood ash and clay]	4
almost the same as	*Amakusa* a porcelain clay	1.5
Kiseto glaze	*ōdo*	2
		(by weight)

This is an interesting glaze with dark yellow (or brown) streaks in yellow (or dark yellow).

After glazing, before it dries, if you draw through the glaze with a bamboo tool and then fire the pot, the drawn lines will fire brown, an interesting effect. The body should be clay that is not too red (not porcelain), and the glaze should not be too thickly applied.

Kamogawa-ishi [an iron and manganese bearing stone]:

Ao-soba [teadust] glaze:	*Kamogawa-ishi*	30
	dobai	20
	warabai [rice straw ash] or *momibai*	50
		(S.K. 6–7)

The cooling must be slow. Body: porcelain or not too red clay

Black raku:	*Kamogawa-ishi*	100
	shiratama	20
		(S.K. 6–7)

This must be cooled rapidly. It would be even better to take out the hot pieces with tongs and immerse them in water. Body: rough clay or clay with grog added.

Isubai:

	S.K. 10–11	S.K. 8
isubai	25	25

Amakusa	75	40
chōseki [feldspar]		35

This makes a good glaze for blue-and-white porcelain.

Mitsu-ishi (a type of kaolin):

mitsu-ishi	10
tō-no-tsuchi	3

This is a good white slip for raku.

Stoneware white slip:

	I	II
mitsu-ishi	44	31
keiseki	33	32
chōseki	23	15
gairome [ball clay]		20
limestone		2

Weak *mitsu-ishi* alone will suffice (or add a little *chōseki*).

Seger cones:

I added Nos. 1 and 9 for the following reasons.

For the stoneware glaze firing (for instance, when firing S.K. 8), only these cones are set

When No. 1 falls (when firing 8–10), the glaze has just begun to melt. It is the most important time. Before melting, the glaze surface becomes rough. At this point, if there is too much smoke, the carbon in the smoke will enter the glaze, and if the glaze melts in that state, it becomes greyish. Thus, until the glaze melts at No. 1, keep the fire as low as possible. When the glaze melts at No. 1, keep a reducing atmosphere for a while, then fire neutral. Setting up No. 1 as a warning avoids problems.

No. 9 is in case of overfiring. Up to cone 8, it is hard to know the extent of overfiring.

05a (1000° C.) glaze:

	I	II
red lead	50.7	91
feldspar	16.2	
Amakusa	16.2	
quartz	15.5	32
limestone	7.7	18
borax (calcined)		14

If it is strong, add red lead and borax; if weak, add quartz, *amakusa*, etc.

For other S.K. 8 glazes:

Dobai glaze:

dobai	3
Amakusa	2
chōseki	5

White Hagi glaze:

dobai	3
chōseki	3
warabi	4

Kinyo glaze:

Add 1% *gosu* to this.

I have spent ¥21.08 to date.

The *gosu* test, *hera*, etc. will be sent the day after tomorrow.

S. Hamada

Leach:

Later a letter came asking if it was possible to consider him coming with me to England as my helper in starting a semi-Oriental type of pottery. This decision did not lie with me entirely but with those who had invited me to come to Cornwall. I wrote and asked whether I might bring a good Japanese assistant, and they agreed to it.

It may occur to some readers that it was strange that Hamada wanted to go to England with me. They will not realize that with the increasing freedom after the restoration of the emperor of Japan (1868) and the later formation of the constitution upon a European model, the desire to explore the rest of the world and its cultures, in a people cut off for 250 years, was profound. Hamada's wish, therefore, was not so unnatural; moreover, as he had been impressed by my work at Abiko, especially my attempts at emulating the friendly, eighteenth-century rural English Toft ware tradition in raku techniques, it is not surprising that he wanted to find out more about its origins.

One day during a firing, at about midnight, Hamada's three old mentors turned up. I was a little surprised—they were very nice, quiet, easy, and I came quickly to the conclusion that they had come to look me over to see if I was a suitable kind of person with whom the young Hamada might go abroad. I rather think I met with their approval. At any rate, from that moment my wife and I were able to begin thinking about getting not only our own but also Hamada's reservations to England.

Hamada:

I think it was during Leach's last year—when he was working with the kiln Seiki Kuroda had built after the Abiko kiln burned down—it happened to be the Year of the Monkey, by the Japanese zodiac; I think it was a request from Kuroda to have something made with a design of the three monkeys, see, hear, and speak no evil. Leach found it very difficult to do three monkeys; he had never done it before. I saw the result and was quite impressed at how well and intricately thought out it was. Another thing was the sundial—this also surprised me very much; I never thought that a sundial could be made of pottery, just as in the same way I was surprised with spoons that Leach made. Such ideas would never occur to a Japanese, I felt. Hair decorations, of course, the Japanese had done before, but spoons and sundials . . .

Then it was decided that I would go with Leach to England. On the technical side, I could be of help due to my work in Kyoto. In the last year there I made ten thousand test specimens of glaze—five thousand of celadon, three thousand of copper-red, two thousand of tenmoku—all in that one year. They are probably still being used at the institute, because I made one hundred pieces of each test specimen. But one cannot make exact glaze copies. Colours vary with altitude, weather conditions, etc. etc. At this time there was an excellent copyist, named Uno, who came and said, "You people think that the scale is everything, but you can't make good glaze by weighing things that way. The only way to make good glaze is to add pinches of ingredients with your fingers. Why don't you try to fire your weighed glaze together with the one I mix?" I did, I weighed, and I used what Uno had mixed with his senses, with his nose, his experience. Every single time, Uno's glaze was better. The difference was that his mixture was lively. Even if Uno had made small mistakes, his glaze lived. The ones done with the scale and the measures were quite correct and precise; we tried this test many times, but our glazes were dead in comparison with the ones Uno mixed.

This man came into my life at the right moment. He left another very deep impression. Many people criticised Uno because he was a copyist, an imitator, but a man who can do such fine work, who understands his materials so well, cannot be criticised as being merely an imitator. Uno had a marvellous sense of intuition—what the Japanese call *kan*. He could feel immediately; he could guess the correct ingredients and their amounts. It was incredible, really.

Tomimoto and Leach served for me as perfect measures against which I could evaluate myself. In this way I felt that, with the technical experience at the institute with the glazes, making the specimens, and so forth, I could be of some help wherever Leach wanted to build his kiln.

Leach:

I had my last exhibition in Tokyo, and it was a great success, providing enough money to pay for our journey. We set out in the summer of 1920 on the *Kamo Maru* of the Japanese shipping line Nippon Yūsen Kaisha from Yokohama to London. When we got to England, Hamada told me that in saying goodbye to Mr. Iseki, the latter had said to him, "I would have thought you would have preferred to go to China. But on the journey, say at Hong Kong, if you think you have made a mistake, do not hesitate to come back at once, we shall cover your expenses."

Hamada:

I had received two other offers. One was from China, to come and experiment

35

with glazes there. They wanted a Japanese. Another was from a Japanese ceramic company.

I felt that if I went as far away from Japan as possible, to England, the other side of the world, I could observe Japan best. That is what I wanted to do most. Because Leach was so close at that time, I felt that England was the right choice. I discussed it with Iseki, who then wanted to find out what kind of people Leach and Yanagi were. So Iseki went quietly to Abiko to look around and to see, and later went to Leach's kiln in Tokyo in the middle of the night when he was firing the kiln. When Iseki knew that I definitely was going to England, he brought me ¥1,000. The first-class passage was ¥720 in those days, and without a word he just produced ¥1,000 and put it in my pocket. When I returned to Japan, Iseki said, "You will need some pocket money", and again he produced some money for me. He was constantly doing such things. I felt no obligations in receiving it; it was as if I was getting money from my own parents. But I wanted to return that first ¥1,000 I received. It took twenty years to do so. Iseki had borrowed that ¥1,000 to give to me, and he was paying interest on it for those twenty years. He was able to pay back the whole thing just before he died. This I learned after his death. People of his time quite often are made of such stuff.

Leach:

Hamada and I had talked about Malay curries, and when our ship docked at Singapore, he was very anxious to taste one, so we went ashore, my wife, Muriel, preferring to stay on board since she was seven months pregnant. We went from one hotel to another, but nowhere was there any Malay curry. Finally we were told to go round the corner, where we could obtain Arabian food. We went there; it looked shabby, but we were determined to try something adventurous —and we did. The menu was in Arabic, and so one sort of took a pencil, shut one's eyes, and put the point on a spot and ordered that. Each dish that we ordered was hotter than the previous one. I distinctly remember feeling like a music hall minstrel with blackened face and burning lips between ear and ear. After that endurance—stupidity perhaps, but fun—we made our way to Raffles Hotel, which is very famous and which looked down on the cricket-ground where my father was captain for many years. There we cooled off with the aid of sumptuous ice creams.

Onwards across the Indian Ocean we came to Ceylon. Again we went ashore, but this time, if I remember rightly, we took my wife, got a gharry (a kind of box on four wheels drawn by a scarecrow horse) and drove over to Mt. Lavinia— I should think it is about five miles away from the city of Colombo. There we really did have a proper Indian curry such as I have never seen or had since.

Back to the ship and onwards through Suez and then eventually home to London, the East End docks, thousands upon thousands of chimney pots looking extraordinarily dismal.

In London we went to the Thackeray Hotel, where my wife's parents had often stayed, just opposite the British Museum. At last I felt we were back in

England, right in the middle of it with that old, black, semi-Greek building with fat columns. The first thing my wife and I wanted to drink and eat was English tea and muffins; and bless me, in Museum Street there was a little shop that provided just that. We ate until we were satisfied. After eleven years, that night we felt that at last we had come home. From London we went to Cardiff, where my wife's parents lived, and Dr. Hoyle, my father-in-law, was director of the Welsh National Museum. We were only just in time, because a few days later there were indications that my wife was about to give birth; we began to get somewhat anxious, since it was a little premature. All went well, except—if I may say except—instead of a single birth, twin girls arrived whom we called Jessamine and Betty. As all went well and normally, I went to St. Ives with Hamada, where a house in Draycott Terrace looking down over the harbour awaited us.

Hamada:

There I was on a ship on my way to England to make a kiln with Leach in St. Ives. I remember arriving in London, but the strange thing to me at that point was that I had one or two friends in London who came to meet me and to take me to a hotel and so forth, but there was Leach with no one to meet him. Leach had spent years in London, but no one came to the ship to welcome him back. When he left Japan there were hundreds of Japanese who saw him off with tears in their eyes. I was taken to a hotel in Great Portland Street. It was a very fine hotel, but I remember the walls being rather dingy, which was difficult to understand.

I thought it would be a good idea to start my stay in London by taking a bus and seeing the city from the upper deck of the bus. I went from one end of the city to the other. When I was finished with one bus route, I would take another. Then I went to as many museums as I could. There were about ten at that time, including the smaller ones. I went to the British Museum, the Victoria and Albert Museum, and so forth. I remember spending not quite three weeks doing such things. Then I went to St. Ives. Leach and his family were in Cardiff while I was in London.

What astonished me most in London were the excellent museums and galleries all over the city. I had never seen anything so fine. The tradition of having museums and galleries was astonishing. The whole city was very dark and dim in general, but what surprised me again were the glass panes. The windows were always brightly cleaned and clear. Also the brass knobs. Wherever I went, however dingy the room was, the windows and brass were very bright and shining. In Japan at that time, no matter how dirty glass became, it was still brighter and clearer than the shoji paper, and so we never thought of cleaning it.

Later, in 1929, I remember renting a room with Yanagi in London. We had to promise the landlord that the glass windows and the brass knobs would be cleaned at least once a week. What a strange promise to make in renting a room. Also, there were a lot of oil paintings. We took all the pictures down, put them away somewhere in the attic, and redecorated the whole room.

Leach and I arrived in St. Ives together. I remember it was August 24, 1920. Leach had returned to London from Cardiff in order to join me for the trip to St. Ives. Mrs. Leach was still in Cardiff.

The first place we stayed was at Draycott Terrace, overlooking the harbour. On the corner was a handcraft shop where there was a very energetic lady, Miss Welch. The view of the harbour was superb. But the Cornish countryside— stone, stone everywhere, nothing but stone! As if all the skin and flesh were taken away and only the bones remained. England, I had heard, was a soft place, like Oxford, with an abundance of large, generous trees. How in heaven's name did I arrive in such a place where there was nothing soft to be found. The trees were bent and wind-blown. And the jutting rocks. Hard. I did not known at first what to make of it, but the longer I stayed, the more I began to like the place, espe- cially the landscape. As one goes towards Land's End, the country gets better and better. Rather than the soft England, I liked the stern and austere Cornwall much better. I liked the Cotswolds very much at first—the thatched roofs, the soft lines—but in Cornwall they use slate, and the stone walls are rough and massive. Pendeen Manor house, not far from St. Just, I thought especially rugged and good. I hope that the government or the English people will preserve such houses.

Leach:

We began to look around for the two things that potters need most—clay and wood, or fuel. We were told that the only kind of clay known in the locality other than china clay was candle clay, so named because a lump of it was put on the helmets of the tin miners, and into that a candle was stuck to give them light. Taking field-glasses, we began walking round the countryside spying out the land, hoping that we might see a cutting and so find a bed of clay. One day, from a high point known as Trencrom, across the valley we espied a streak of yellowish looking clay in a cutting behind a village called St. Erth. We made our way down to the station there, and outside the station on the road there was some clay that had been dropped from a cart. I picked it up. It looked like a yellowish beach sand, but it was plastic, and I had never seen a plastic sand before. This was rather curious. We went into the village and found the foreman of a small clay-digging company, who told us about it. He said that this sandy clay was used as a moulding material for casting bronze, but, also, that at one time in the past he had dug up a very smooth plastic variety of this yellowish clay in church land nearby. So we went to see the parson, who at that time only asked a price of ten shillings a ton. The clay was about six to eight feet below the sur- face, and, having the permission to dig, within a week we had some samples of this yellowish clay. The first thing to find out when we had a test kiln would be what temperature this clay would stand. I thought it would be like the clay that is used for chimney pots.

We had not got our pottery yet, we had not even decided the site. There were several available, and we chose one on the road that is called the Stennack, leading uphill out of St. Ives to Land's End. It was a strip of land about one hundred yards long and perhaps twenty or thirty yards wide next to the stream of the same name, the Stennack, which means "tin stream".

The next thing was a builder and the plans. Hamada and I were busy talking and discussing what was the best idea for laying out the pottery, and we eventually produced a rough plan. I think it was the surveyor of the town whom we employed and who put it into shape for us. It was passed by the Town Council in due order, and we had a builder and his men start work. Part of the building was open to the rafters, the other part was ceiled for storing pots to dry either from the heat of the room below or from the heat on the slate roof and in the gable area in summer. Some of these ideas were Hamada's, some of them mine; it was really a fifty-fifty situation with nobody being boss, simply one man helping another—that was always our relationship. The material chosen was natural granite, not the first and best class, but a sufficiently good one for a roughish outbuilding. It turned out to be one of the last buildings constructed out of that traditional material in St. Ives.

Hamada:

We investigated two or three sites for a kiln. The reason why the particular spot was chosen where the Leach Pottery is today was because of the adjacent stream, which we felt might prove to be useful.

The site was still cow pasture, and there were many problems of how to clear the area. We had to start from scratch. Once I arrived in St. Ives, I asked around whether there were any local kilns. There were not. There were bread ovens, but they were much too small. I believe it was at nearby Hayle that fire bricks were available. Good fire bricks were found there because a company was experimenting with explosives, so we were able to build a kiln very cheaply. As far as the kiln was concerned, we decided on the climbing kiln. For the clay, we thought of digging on the spot and then washing and sieving it, but it was not satisfactory.

Then we thought of going to a tin mine and finding a slope to determine what had been dug up. We were given permission to investigate a tin mine, but could not tell very well what clay was available. They had candle clay, but plasticity alone would not do. Certain roughness of texture was needed for our work. So every day Leach and I wore our rubber shoes and walked uphill and downhill, looking for proper clay. Going up a hill, I had shorter legs and would be quicker than Leach. He would have an awful time huffing and puffing, but coming down he was much quicker, and I fell behind.

Then one day, on the road before us, we found some red clay that had crumbled from the hillside. It had just enough plasticity and stiffness. We took it home. I made a ball of it and put it before the fire-place. Suddenly it rolled into the fire. We waited to see whether it would explode in the heat of the flames, but it did not. Instead, it made a beautiful biscuit. We knew then that this clay would work very well. The next day we felt we had to trace exactly where this clay came from; in order to do so we went in separate directions to look. We found the hill from which it came right away. Near the site, this clay was used for making metal-casting moulds. It had the quality of withstanding a sudden rise in temperature and not cracking. We decided to use it.

Leach:

The work went on, and we continued discussing the slope of the land and how we must dig a hole for the lower end or ash-pit end of the kiln, which we were going to do on the old Korean and Japanese principle of a sloping or climbing kiln requiring almost no chimney. We found that, as we dug down for the ash pit, water began to come in from the Stennack stream twenty feet away, seeping through rough land that had been formed mainly by debris from the mines further up the hill (called Consols Mines). However, we began to make a foundation; the men worked well, the walls rose, and the building was covered with slate in the traditional Cornish manner, which belonged to the landscape.

One of the men who was working as a casual labourer was called George Dunn. One day when he saw us working clumsily with the long-handled Cornish shovels, he came over and showed Hamada and myself how to use one's knee, usually the left knee, as a fulcrum for pushing and shovelling the clay with one movement. I was grateful for that.

The time came when the new building was nearly finished. We had a date fixed the next week for its completion and after that we were going to work indoors, making our own cupboards with asbestos sheeting, benches, and so forth, as we thought fit for our purpose. One morning we walked up from Draycott Terrace together, up the long Stennack, discussing what we were going to do during the day. There, where we expected to find the place empty, stood George Dunn. He wasn't five feet high and was as bright as a button. I said, "Hello George, what are you doing here? I thought you'd finished." He held out his hand and replied, "Cap'n, put it there, I'm staying." I paused, and I shook his hand, and he stayed until he died. Not only that, but he gave us all that he had to give.

His was a real loyalty, which came to a climax once, years later. (Hamada wasn't there, but I think it worthwhile telling in passing.) We had a fire when the roof of the kiln shed caught alight for the same reasons as in my previous fire in Japan. I had not learned my lesson sufficiently—the heat had accumulated in a closed-in area. George noticed that the insurance company paid up; it was a normal claim.

Later, when he learned that I was planning to leave St. Ives and go to Dartington Hall in Devonshire he was upset. One day it came to a head. I was sitting on a bench and he came and sat beside me. He put his hand on my knee and said, "Cap'n, I'm afeared for 'ee." I said, "What are you afraid of?" "Money," he replied, tapping his trouser pocket. I said that it was all right, I could manage. "I'm afeared for 'ee," he repeated, then he whispered, "Now you give me the word and I'll put a match to 'un anytime." He meant burn the whole place down and get the insurance. Well, it may not be moral, but it was an extraordinarily brave, well-meaning offer according to traditional Cornish ideas. That was the sort of man he was.

He not only offered his own labour but brought his family in too. It was a personal affection. When he was threatened with expulsion from the old cottage he lived in at the end of the land, I built a cottage for him and gave him the use of it at a nominal rental. He had never had anybody in his life do anything like that, I suppose. Well, anyway, this is my rationalization of the situation and that is what happened. Hamada liked him too. You could not help liking the man, he was so warm, so full of life. At a football match, from a quarter of a mile away his was the dominant voice shouting for his side against all comers.

There were many things that we had to do at the beginning. We had a series of discussions concerning clay, glazes, and so on. We found one use for that yellowish clay mentioned before. We put up a small, temporary stoneware kiln for testing purposes and found that when mixed with china clay obtained locally it produced a body that could be used successfully for our slipware. It was quite a nice clay and withstood the temperature of up to 1,100° C. quite easily. I do not suppose it had been used for that purpose before; all we had heard about this yellow clay was that it was used in the building of the waterfront of a nearby fishing port, Newlyn. The granite surfaces were backed up by layers of plastic clay, which was comparatively impervious to water and therefore strengthened the granite-faced dockside. So we had some local clay, but we had to get ball clay, which stands high temperatures and is plastic, from Devonshire or Dorset. We also got fire clay from below the coal seams of the Midlands and rather depended on it. It had a wholemeal bread-like quality, very pleasant in texture.

Here I think I ought to touch a bit on the building of our traditional Korean or Japanese stoneware climbing kiln. That was something entirely new in the West—as far as I know no such kiln had ever been built before in the Western world. In our three-chamber climbing kiln each chamber measured six feet in height, six feet in width, and four feet from front wall to back wall. It was the use of the slope (a forty-degree angle) that created the right kind of draught and enabled the potter to fire one chamber after another. The fire enters, meets with a wall of saggers, which forces it up and over the top and down into the space at the back; and then it goes through passages in the lower part of the wall into the next chamber and so on, so that each chamber can be varied in temperature or atmosphere at will. Several temperatures can be used in different chambers if one so wishes. It is very common in the East to use the last chamber of all not for glazed ware but for firing biscuit; the last chamber would, in that case, require no further stoking.

Hamada's reaction against the over-scientific and technical approach to potting in his schooling caused him to be anxious to use materials straight from nature—he knew quite well how traditional potters of the past had done so. At his suggestion we actually dug for ourselves some of that china clay, with its impurities of unchanged granite material including feldspar and fragments of quartz. This mixture was hammered into moulds, making blocks with which we built the kiln. We probably put some ball clay into it at that stage, and fire clay, which both withstand very high temperatures. (Plastic ball clay was employed in making most pots in the industrial area of the Five Towns, where it was sold in the form of lumps of clay and carried on barges. The lumps of clay looked like footballs, hence the name.) At any rate, we built a kiln, which only cost us time and labour and which gave us some good results. The kiln certainly brought us close to nature, so close that we had several mishaps, and it eventually deteriorated to such an extent that cracks developed through which you could push your hand from one chamber to another.

We fired it with wood, and neither of us had been thoroughly trained in wood-firing to a high temperature or, for that matter, in drying and cutting wood—I think that first kiln was taken by storm, so to speak. Our mistakenly extravagant use of wood deposited ash on the walls, which did not help the kiln's condition. It did give us some early pots that were quite good, and we exhibited them. The last firing Hamada ever did in that kiln was one of the best that I remember—effects for which you might have waited twenty years in vain, though it was responsible for most of the damage to the old kiln. So finally we had to build another, and this time we had the help of an old school associate of Hamada's, Tsuneyoshi Matsubayashi. His knowledge of climbing and other kilns in Japan was considerable and a great advantage to us. Matsubayashi was very much a technician; he had a well-regulated mind. The second climbing kiln was a great improvement on the first, though built on similar lines. It is still used today, though, of course, it has been more or less rebuilt over the years.

Hamada:

I had brought my Japanese wheel to St. Ives because I was inexperienced with any other kind. Then there was the matter of bringing bamboo for making tools. What I did not think to bring were long split bamboo poles to be used for supports for making the roof and arches of a kiln. Actually what was needed was fresh, green bamboo that would bend easily. Dry bamboo is harder and brittle. I felt that I had not thought thoroughly enough before departing. However, we were able to use curved staves from large barrels used in St. Ives to pack salted herring. We needed saggers, and the clay we used was so coarse that, unless we were careful, the skin on our hands was chafed off.

Leach:

In addition we had a round kiln, about a yard in diameter inside and a yard in height. Beneath the floor was a fire-mouth and passage into which wood was fed. Big logs, which are slow burning, were used first to heat the raw wares gradually. Though dry, clay nevertheless contains chemically combined water, which, if heated too quickly, may cause the pots to explode. We also fired our glazed raku ware in this same round kiln, which was also used for the somewhat greater heat of English slipware, about 1,000° C. This slipware was packed on perforated triangular shelves, tier upon tier, leaving something like a two-inch gap on the outside for the flames to rise to the top. The temperature at the top was a full one hundred degrees lower than at the bottom, and it was on the top shelf that the raku ware was fired.

Raku needs a very low temperature, about the lowest used in glazed pottery.

A raku kiln is fired to about 750° C., which is a bright red heat. We fired this kiln once a week, partly with the intention of having the pottery open for the public that afternoon, and put up a notice to that effect. Any visitors during the summer could come and spend the afternoon painting their designs on pots, which we provided in a simple biscuited form, could see us glaze the pots there and then, dry them round the top of the kiln, removing a few of the top bricks that covered the dome so that we could push these pots with long-handled tongs into the red heat. It did happen sometimes that they did not get sufficiently pre-heated on the top, the water in the walls of the pots formed steam, and there was an explosion. Since the lower part of the kiln was stacked with slipware, such occurrences were rather disastrous, because bits of the raku pots that burst with a bang fell onto the glazed ware below. We took precautions, but, even so, this did happen occasionally. I was nearly always the one who put the pots in and took them out, and it was quite an afternoon.

The people who came to these raku sessions in the early days had to manage with only the help of our brief written instructions regarding the pigments (they did not use glazes)—how thick they should be and how they should be put on, what should be avoided—and this led to many errors. They put on all sorts of designs. I think the commonest was a cat drawn as a ball with a tail at one end and a smaller ball for the head with two ears and five whiskers (two on one side and three on the other), sitting on a wall. St. Ives, of course, has the famous jingle:

> As I was going to St. Ives
> I met a man with seven wives,
> Each wife had seven sacks,
> Each sack had seven cats,
> Each cat had seven kits,
> Kits, cats, men, and wives,
> How many were going to St. Ives?

which we ourselves sometimes put on those early slipware pots, engraving them through the white slip down to the reddish body. Those pots did not cost much, and the visitor who came in fine weather could get tea provided by my wife. They would buy perhaps three pots and try experiments with them, pretty ghastly as a rule, and this brought us in about fifty pence apiece. It did not pay; but it did bring the fact to the notice of visitors to St. Ives that there was a pottery about three-quarters of a mile above the town on the Land's End road. So it brought people into our show-rooms, and they came back year after year.

One thing I have not mentioned yet is the wood we used to fire the kiln. Where were we to get the wood that we were determined to use? Wood is by far the best of fuels; its direct attack on glaze surfaces is not damaging but improving, whereas coal, with the amount of sulphur in it, or even gas or oil do not help the glaze so much, nor form the thin natural glazing on the bare parts of the pot exposed to the wood ash and flame. There were no real forests here—the north-west wind simply swept bare our part of the exposed leg of England called Cornwall. It is only on the south coast of the peninsula, the lee side, that there is some growth, and we obtained some of our earlier cuttings of pine wood there. But it always was and always is a problem to get wood in our locality in Cornwall. We managed to, by hook or crook, from various sources. From the first we were faced with this problem, and during our expeditions to find clay we were always on the lookout for wood as well.

Above St. Ives there rises a structure that looks like a church spire, but is nothing of the sort. It is a memorial to a mayor of former centuries and is a landmark for the fishing boats. All around it the ground is densely covered with huge rhododendrons. That wood was being picked up by the villagers in the locality and taken away. It struck me one day that in those woods there were a lot of black pines that had died after about thirty years of growth. They were rather inaccessible because of the denseness of the rhododendron undergrowth, which could also be used by us as fuel. Could I not make an offer to the Great Western Railway to whom it belonged and get a price quotation that was feasible? I did, and they sent a man down; we went out and marked the trees and for twenty pounds got all the dead wood. I was rather cunning about it, I think— I realized that the preliminary cutting of paths through the rhododendron to those dead trees produced a lot more wood, so that eventually for twenty pounds we had bought about two hundred tons, and it would cost us about one hundred pounds to get it to the pottery. The whole one hundred yards of our land at the edge of the road was piled with heaps and heaps of mainly rhododendron wood, which lasted us, I think, at least two years, perhaps three. So that is how we started with wood, though rhododendron was only partly suitable because it was twisted, which made it difficult to feed into the side of the big kiln, but it was excellent for the stoking of the smaller biscuit and raku kiln.

Hamada:

I was surprised to know that it cost nearly one hundred pounds to cart the wood over a distance of only one mile. I was more surprised to know that it cost less to saw the wood by motor than to employ workers, who demanded high wages. The next problem was to split the wood. I knew the type of Japanese axe that would do the job and went to a blacksmith to have one made, with an example made in clay to copy. He did not know how much it would weigh in iron, and in fact it weighed seven pounds—so heavy it would break your arm. Then Leach suggested we make use of the water power of the stream that runs through the property, hoping to find something that would cut the wood. We borrowed a machine saw, but this attempt failed. Somehow or other we sawed the wood into about two-foot lengths and then split the lengths with small axes and wedges. With George Dunn helping, we had in the end three years' worth of firewood.

Leach:

Rather soon after our arrival the members of the Old Cornwall Society founded by Robert Morton Nance, who was the first friend I made upon coming from

Japan and whose son Dicon eventually married my daughter Eleanor, took Hamada and myself to see Pendeen Manor, which was built in the reign of Elizabeth I. The four upright posts of a bed caught Hamada's eye. The tops of the four-inch-thick posts were chamfered, with identical diagonal saw cuts making a pattern. He did a drawing from which he made his own bed out of pine firewood of that four-inch diameter. The material he used was dead wood from Steeple Hill, and although he, and later I, kept it for years, eventually the Cornish woodworms beat us and it was burned in the kiln with the last of our wood from that source. I cannot forget that bed—somehow it was old English and at the same time Hamada. He is one of those men who stamp their personality on whatever they do. Years later I observed him instructing a master builder in Japan, drawing with his finger on the wet surface of his potters' wheel just how he wanted the proportions and bevels of a window under construction in his farmhouse. He can draw very well with ink or paper, pen or brush. Hamada's spontaneous drawing is expressive of material and form at its most basic level. It is a shorthand—but more, it captures the essence of an object clearly and vividly.

And then there was the room in which Hamada lived in the pottery, and the manner in which he lived. There used to be a small room, the walls of which were taken away in after years. It was about eight by ten feet, and there was room for a chest of drawers, a table and chair, a bed, and nothing else. The bed took up rather a lot of room, not so much because of its width or length but because its rough wood contained no nails and the pegs of the joints projected about three or four inches from the bed frame. There was no bathroom, just the sink and a basin in the pottery section; a table and a chair were beside the corner fire-place. He used to come over to us sometimes for a bath or to the house opposite, where Edgar Skinner, our secretary, lived. His life was very simple, and it was not entirely English or Oriental but an adaptation of the human being Hamada to his Cornish environment. Eventually that young potter became one of those rare artists and, in his case, craftsmen, who belong to two hemispheres. He cooked for himself on a gas ring, but he did not always make Japanese food. He tried to grow some Japanese vegetables from seed, occasionally with success, and Edgar Skinner showed him how to grow English vegetables. His kind of living and thinking put value on simplicity and on absence of possessions —Hamada in St. Ives preferred to travel light.

Hamada:
When the firewood came, Leach and I had more spare time, and I took the saw and began to make my own bed with it. I chose only the curved wood. The working area of the pottery was L-shaped, and Leach and I had our wheels one in each corner. The wet box, which is still there today, was on the right side as you went in, on the short leg of the L.

Leach:
At the farther end, on the other side of the L, there is still a place today where

45

we say "Hamada slept here" because that is where his bed was. Only in the last few years did the factory inspectors force us to put a cement floor there in place of the wooden floor. In the angle of this L is the fireplace where he cooked.

Hamada:

I would eat bread in the morning and bread in the afternoon, but I wanted to have some rice in the evening at least. I got a pound bag of rice, but the closest I could find to Japanese rice was Javanese. I washed it, as the Japanese wash rice, and put enough water in it, but the pot was too light, so I had to weigh down the lid with a brick to allow some pressure inside the pot when it began to boil. As soon as I heard the sound "chking-chking" I knew the rice was ready, and the first time that I opened the lid I could see that there were just enough holes in the surface of the rice. I knew that it was good rice. I served it to my fisherman friend, Old Basset, and thereafter the rice pot was called the "chking-chking" pot. Everyone liked the rice; it was firmer than the kind eaten in England, but all thought it was very fine in flavour.

In those early days there was not any overall organization in the pottery, we did what we were enthusiastic about. A great deal was lost in the firing. We were learning our standards, if we could find them, and we lost between twenty and thirty percent of the pots that we made. There were all kinds of losses; accidents, dunting, skipped glazes, deformed shapes, fallen saggers, all sorts of things. Besides that, after a firing, even a good one, we would go through the pots and take out a certain number of our own that we did not like, put them up on the keel of an old boat next to the river, and when we were disgusted with our own work, or wanted a little exercise, we would get a rock or two to throw at these pots—it was a grand, clean sound when they broke and fell into the stream.

Leach came to the workshop from his house about two miles away—first on foot and then by motorbike. His English life was governed by appointments and time. He had no opportunity to settle down to throwing and decorating. In the morning he did shopping in the town on his way to work, ordering meat and vegetables or taking shoes for repair. When he finished writing letters, it was about noon. I recall the figure of Leach as he went up and down in the small town of St. Ives, holding a little notebook filled with lists and crossing out each item as he finished it.

Frequently he longed for the days he spent in Japan, when he could immerse himself in work, and lamented that he would not be able to become a perfect Englishman again. Yet he settled down firmly in his native land and followed his determination to perform the job that he called "meeting of East and West".

Leach:

The relationship between Hamada and myself was really good. He was in an experimental stage, and whilst he was thus engaged, I was able to give myself over to form and decoration. I do not remember a flow, exactly, of pots from him, either stoneware, raku, or slipware; I remember experimental ones that were successful. He did not exhibit them until his third year in England, and then it was in Old Bond Street at the Paterson Gallery. Old Mr. Paterson took to Hamada, and he had two shows there before he left England. So he left me the legacy, so to speak, of the Paterson Gallery, where I also had a show later on.

In the workshop it was very quiet; over meals, especially supper, we would talk and relax and discuss all aspects of potting—what it meant to be a thinking artist-potter of today, in contrast to the potters of most epochs of the past all over the world; part of a group that produced things scarcely thought about as art for its own sake but considered as enjoyable, right things for normal daily use. I was trained in art; Hamada in pottery technology. We were not folk potters, nor were we simple country folk, like those who made the best English medieval pots (or their counterparts in the Far East)—we were artist-potters and, as such, our horizons had begun to be all horizons. We endlessly discussed all aspects of potting, and we admired what is in folk art and nowhere else. We talked of the possibility, so long after the beginning of the industrial revolution, of finding people who would be willing to go through training and to continue making pots for the rest of their lives. Anyone out of industry was so conditioned by industrial thought as to be less than useful to us. The artist-potter cannot pretend to be a folk potter; the potter of today is inevitably travelled, educated, and conscious, even self-conscious. Hamada, and to some extent Michael Cardew, are examples of a just balance between the two. They are certainly not unconscious, but neither has been defeated by self-consciousness.

Coming from the East, Hamada's East, we were on the lookout for quality in a sense that was not recognized in England at that time—it was seen as failure, as bad material. Hardness, whiteness, and translucency were looked upon as the ideal. We brought from the East, Hamada and I, a new concept of quality in pots—of textures, of quiet colours.

We were applying to pots an appreciation of nature, of the natural effects of raw materials. Good quality in pottery was hitherto associated with purity, with expensive refinement, and we were challenging the Victorian concept of good taste. The general reaction was that our work was dull; the European could not distinguish between one brown and another, or between one texture and another. However, ideas were changing—old Chinese tombs were being excavated, and for the first time work from the Sung dynasty was being seen. The Sung pots, mainly stoneware, were like remelted rock, full of impurities and very close to nature. Their gentle colours and warm textures were a far cry from the decorated porcelains of Staffordshire and Derby. Hamada and I were consciously using impure materials that were considered by the Westerner to be second-rate or faulty. Such materials were thought of as fit only for certain purposes, such as in the kitchen or garden, for wares considered far too homely to be thought of as art. We delighted in the natural subtleties wood ash and other impure materials can have when fired at stoneware temperatures.

Let me now turn to an ash glaze we used. Kenkichi Tomimoto had translated from the Chinese a seventeenth- or eighteenth-century document describing the use of bracken ash glaze for porcelaineous wares. One autumn day some of us were climbing the slopes of Rosewall, the first of a series of rolling hills between

47

us and Land's End, and noticed that the slopes were covered with bracken shoulder high and as brown as the tobacco in a smoker's pouch. It must have been a good year, because the bracken did not always grow so profusely. A few days later we foregathered and cut great amounts of bracken and piled it on clean ground. We burned it slowly, using a watering can to keep it from burning too quickly into a white ash, since we wanted to retain a quantity of black carbon in it to produce a black, or blackish, ash and consequently a reduced effect in the glaze when fired. We had to leave the burning pile overnight, since it was still glowing. Next morning it was cool enough to gather into gunny bags and take down to the pottery. After washing and sieving it, we mixed it with feldspar and, I think, quartz. It made a creamy white, big-crackled glaze, which we have never since equalled. It was velvety white, it took pigment on its surface with gentleness, it did not look mechanized, it was hard and it was soft at the same time. We attempted that same effect in successive years, but never got it again. The reason for this was partly the season in which the dried vegetable was taken from the hills, and partly, no doubt, the amount of salt in the sea air that had dried onto the bracken. Many people have commented upon these primitive, simple methods of tradition; it may be seen, as Hamada pointed out, that they are not so simple after all. One pot done in this glaze was the original fish bottle (as I call it), which is in the Victoria and Albert Museum, but heavily mended.

These are hints of the excitement in making glazes. Some people become very obsessed with glaze composition—many get carried away into certain byways in the journey of a potter in his training. There are people who get enamoured of copper-reds; I have met several who spent their life on them. The Chinese gave literary names to glaze colours and pursued every nuance of effect. They also had many different names for crackle in glazes. By industrial standards, crackle is just a fault and is called crazing. It does not completely prevent water from going through the surface, and underneath, the clay may not be fully vitrified, in which case the pot is liable to leave round marks and stains on piano tops and goodness knows where else, and may even leak. I remember when Hamada and I visited a great collector of art, George Eumorfopoulos; Mrs. Eumorfopoulos in a very kind manner took me to her piano and showed me one of those irremovable rings. She had put one of my pots filled with flowers on the top, and that was what happened. I had sold it without testing it and did not know it was still porous. I was humbled but not put to shame. This is the kind of thing one has to go through. One has to learn by errors, and sometimes it is rather difficult because you may have to give up beauty for the sake of utility, and that the artist in a potter hates to do—he is so much in love with beauty.

Hamada:
What we needed was ash for glaze. A black ash was required. We first burned bracken, but it required so much for so little that it was not practical—a whole roomful of dried bracken made a bucketful of ash. One of us had the idea of going to a kipper factory, where they smoked the fish, and I remember being teased by

the girls when we went there. It did not matter, because I did not understand a word they were saying. We were overpowered by the smell of the place, but never mind, we wanted the ash from the sawdust they were using for smoking the fish. The heads and tails of the fish fell into the sawdust, so we had a stinking mess to sieve and wash to kill the smell. Not only this, but the kipper factory burned a load of sawdust for only one night, so that much of it was not completely burned—it was really crude stuff.

In order to make black glaze it is better to have rougher ash, that is, a mixture of clay and the darker part of the ash with all its impurities. So after the kiln had been fired, we would get the cruder pine ash and sieve it to make glaze. We added iron to this; generally five percent is enough, but for a really good black glaze perhaps from ten to twelve percent iron is added. This would make a good tenmoku and is also good for celadon. Little by little we prepared the different kinds of glazes to be used for our work. In the meantime, the saggers began to bend and the kiln became too deformed to use. We had to overcome all sorts of problems in those first three years.

Leach:

It was through Hamada and his reaction against the Germanic scientific and theoretic training that he received at his pottery school that I realized the superiority of the natural processes employed by early potters all over the world. From him also I received a glimpse of the condition of mind as well as insight into the practical techniques of the earlier Oriental potters. This exchange between us was not based upon theory before practice but upon practice before theory in the pursuit of that which we considered beautiful and true. I had no real training in science, whereas Hamada had, and he was now at my elbow. At second hand I learned something of the principles involved, only by using intuition rather than textbooks. He did not like the coldness of the analytical approach; he got sick of textbooks. It took him away from the sheer experience of man and clay and fire into a world of theory before practice, and he and many of his Oriental friends held this as a bad mark against European culture. They say that Europeans go to theory before practice, and that is what has upset the aesthetic standards of Europe to a large extent. They say that we have always put intellect before intuition, but at the expense of that which speaks from one man's heart to another, which is the nature of art. All this Hamada taught me; in fact I have learned not only from Hamada but from Buddhism more than I have learned from the West about such things. In later years I realized how strongly earlier Christianity also had put the heart before the head.

Hamada and I had both acquired a background of Japanese quiet and austerity, and the things we made reflected this. People who came to our show-room would say, when, occasionally, they were bold enough to do so, "Well, to tell you the truth Mr. Leach, I do think your pots are very dull, haven't you got any blue?" I would reply, "Do you mean a really bright blue like laundry bluing?" They would say, "Yes, yes, that's right", and I would reply, "I'm sorry, but it's not the kind of brightness I care for in pots and I don't do it. It

49

can be done, but I prefer not to. I have another kind of preference after being in the Far East". Hamada would not say much, but you could see from a slight twinkle in his eye that he approved of that kind of response to a public demand. After blue, they liked nasturtium orange, or bright apple green, and it was years before we could get people to appreciate the quiet innate kind of colours of the raw materials themselves and of nature in its quieter moods—a certain amount of freckle of iron in the clay or a tinge of grey-green in a celadon. England had become confused by the loud proclamations of science and the bad "court" taste of Victoria's era.

I remember a few of Hamada's raku pots. I still have some. One that I like particularly is a very lovely ochre red done in that sandy clay we first picked up off the ground near St. Erth station. The clay is very porous, but it took the thin white slip engobe, and Hamada decorated the piece with sgraffito. It was one of those lovely effects that I value very much, and it began to tell me of the quality of form, temperament, and rhythm that was this man Hamada's natural expression. Very close to nature, very wholemealy, with a kind of weightiness and strength—broad-footed. It was of the nature of the man who made it.

Now let us turn to English slipware. It developed out of medieval lead-glazed pots, which I think were nobler. A change took place when the centre of the village became the pub instead of the church. Sociability began to take the place of religion. The core of belief that was expressed in the church or cathedral turned into the good-fellowship overflow of social life in public houses. Belief that held the people together in dreams of truth and beauty found a lesser head-quarters. This happened, of course, about the time of Henry VIII and Elizabeth I, and it did not destroy the work made by people in clay, but changed it. It became "Hail fellow well met, when this is down we'll have another", as is en-graved on an eighteenth-century pitcher.

The slipware clay was the red clay of which bricks and chimney pots are made; this is found in most countries all over the world—the commonest form of clay. It was decorated as a rule by dipping it in or pouring over it a white slip. You could deal with it when it was still wet to the surface, half-dried. You could hold it as you would a lump of cheese and comb it while still wet with a wooden comb —soft of tooth—with a swift movement of the hand. You might make gentle marks through to the red body, filling an otherwise empty space that felt in-complete. Alternatively, you could wait until the slip was damp-dry to the touch and engrave lettering, preferably with a chisel-headed point used rather like a quill, the lines thin in one movement and thick in another.

We regained perhaps eighty percent of the old techniques of slipware decora-tion, of the use of white slip over a red body and a middle temperature. Hamada loved it too—in fact he took this tradition back to Japan and made use of it translated into stoneware. He also passed it on to an old Japanese pottery (the Fujina Pottery), which happened to be using lead glaze, one of the only ones in Japan. The influence of English potting there continues today.

It was exciting work. Hamada has sometimes used English shapes and even trail-glazed in the slip manner, but he has never just copied—there is all the world of difference between imitation and inspiration. There are, for example, moulded dishes made by slices of clay placed over a hump mould, pressed down all over with the palms of the hands, then cut off with a wire at the edge and presently taken off gently by reversing the mould and releasing the bowl or platter. The question was, how had they decorated some of these with what is called feathering (trailed white slip run through at right angles by a feather point)? We realized, not immediately, that it could not have been done on the curved surface; the lines would not have remained parallel. So it dawned on either Hamada or myself one day that obviously it had been done on the flat slice of clay before it was pressed on the mould. It was in such ways that we learned much of what had been lost; these things were not recorded in any books we ever came across, and none of the museum people were able to tell us. We found an American book on the exported English slipware of the eighteenth century, and hither and thither we began to get some bits of information and piece them together and rediscover by the sheer common sense workshop approach the old techniques otherwise liable to be lost forever. We later learned that this technique was probably still alive in remote areas of northern England, but, being used for ordinary cooking wares, it was not recognized by the museum people.

Hamada's approach was from an Oriental background, contrasting with my training at an English art school, which no doubt owed much of its background to Renaissance thought. I learned to think in terms of line—line that is drawn with something derived from the stylus. Hamada's background was one of a greater closeness to wild nature, to long, soft brushes, to wind bending the grass, to spontaneous broken line with behind it the stern discipline of Chinese writing, and, perhaps most importantly, to asymmetric composition and rhythm. This field of beauty was not appreciated when we first started in Cornwall, and I felt dumbfounded at the remarks that were made by visitors to our show-room. I said to myself, "What am I going to do in this country if people have no sympathy towards the loveliness that I learned in the East?" However, Hamada was a warm companion, and we shared our difficulties.

Hamada:
Someone ordered a panel to decorate the wall of a room. We used our local clay and raku glaze, which we had brought from Japan. The piece came out all right, the glaze and colour were also good, but the panel seemed strange when hung on that stone wall of an English house. It lacked something. The soft raku glaze colours blend well in a Japanese room of wood, paper, grass, and clay, but it did not harmonize with a room of stone walls and glass windows; the surroundings were too hard.

Another time, Leach placed a Chinese clay figure, which he had brought back with him, in an English room. It appeared cold, hard, and different from what we saw in Japan. Then the effects of the Japanese paper shoji screens came to mind. The glow from the paper screens and the bright light from glass windows are decidedly different. I made a screen with paper I had purchased in Korea

51

before coming to England. Then Leach attached red strings to it in Korean style. When we hung the paper screen before the window, the light was softened, bringing out the gentle swells of the cheeks and the curves of the Chinese figure. Without such light and the appropriate materials surrounding it, raku ware was not satisfactory in England.

We had to try something else. We decided to experiment with galena glazes of the traditional English earthenware. First we added a small amount of the clay we had found—it was very sandy—to the galena powder and fired to what we guessed to be about 1,000° C. We made two or three pieces, and, to our surprise, the glaze was successful on the first try. At last we had something indigenous—the earth was indigenous and the glaze was indigenous. We decided to work with these materials.

Even before we built a big kiln, we decided to try to make large platters with these materials and loaded the little biscuit kiln with as many as possible. We competed with each other in making these large dishes. I often beat Leach in making bigger ones. We had great fun competing with each other in this way. I would do the throwing, and Leach would turn. The ones that I carried back to Japan were thrown by me and turned by Leach.

We had many difficulies. The kiln was very small, and we crammed it with dishes. The platters would stick together, and often the stilts would move about in the heat or fuse to the pieces, leaving scars. There is one piece that I still have —a reindeer dish by Leach—that is excellent. Many people still come to borrow it for exhibitions. What I learned from all this is the fact that something as simple as raku may be right for one place but does not fit everywhere. A great lesson to me was that if a thing is not indigenous, it just does not work. The clay and the glaze must come from the area in which one is working.

An everyday kitchen item in Cornwall was a pitcher, which came in many sizes, from little milk pitchers to large, bucket-sized water pitchers. It was something like the English medieval pottery in finish and tone. It was of red clay, dipped in white slip around the mouth, and usually glazed inside only. I was very much interested to see these pitchers displayed in kitchen-ware shops, and visited the pottery where they were made in the town of Truro, about twenty-five miles from St. Ives.

There they used old hand-cranked, pulley-driven wheels and simple bottle (updraught) kilns, more than six feet in diameter and about fifteen feet in height. They used neither shelves nor saggers but piled up the pitchers in the kiln, using pieces of slate as shelves and supports. They used bundles of gorse as fuel. The clay was very sticky, and throwing was fast. Shapes were just cut from the wheel with wire. After waiting for some time for a pitcher body to dry, they stuck a handful of clay onto the rim and, with much skill, pulled it out as if it were toffee and made it into a handle. Glaze was made, I was told, by simply adding proper clay to powdered lead ore (galena). I felt as if I was seeing the slipware, which impressed me most among British ceramics in the Victoria and Albert and other museums, being made before my eyes. I was impressed by everything I saw and heard.

In St. Ives I gradually became accustomed to the life there while spending busy days during the construction of the pottery and building the kiln. I began to associate with the people in the neighbourhood. One day, a man who lived across the street invited me to tea. There I could not believe my eyes when I saw large dishes, measuring about one and a half feet across, with black backgrounds and simple white stripe designs. I was simply amazed by them. I thought they were made by alternating white clay and red clay layers, resembling plywood in cross section. But when I looked at the bottom, the clay was only one colour, which meant that the dishes were not made by combining two different colour clays in this manner. I could not understand. I asked Leach, and he did not know either.

St. Ives was then known as a herring port. At its height, it was said that the port handled a catch of more than two million herring a night. The people would cut open the fish and smoke them on poles to make kippers. When the season came, red-haired women would come to the town from the north to work in the kippering plants. The women would stay in St. Ives until the herring began to move north again, then they would return to their homes in Wales and Scotland. The surplus herring were packed into barrels and salted and shipped to the inland areas of Germany and Russia to become the major protein source for the farmers there. The local farmers in St. Ives would buy what was left as fertilizer for their fields. This, of course, attracted the seagulls. On fine days the birds would flock to the fields and break up the soil while feeding on the herring fertilizer. When we saw the birds, we went out to the field nearby and gathered many shards of old pottery from the broken soil. This pottery was the same kind of slipware I had seen at the neighbour's house. From the number of these pieces we concluded that the ware was once used extensively. Studying these fragments, we gathered that the original shapes were circular or rectangles with rounded corners, and that a mould instead of a wheel was used. Diameters ranged from about eight to twenty inches. The larger ones had notched rims, probably for strength.

Picking up the fragments and carefully scrutinizing them, we discovered bands of white clay laid one after another in black clay ground. The effect was similar to inlay, but it is impossible to arrange inlay so widely and flatly. Some fragments contained lines of feathered patterns, while others had simple white patterns in the blackish clay. The colour of the glaze appeared yellow; the red clay body was coated with black slip. In cross section, the white did not simply lie on the surface, but penetrated deeply, as in inlay. Galena glaze was applied only on the inside, and the firing temperature was relatively low. We thought there must be a way to reproduce this method and tried many times, but always missed the mark.

Time passed quickly. My second autumn in St. Ives arrived. Blackberries began to ripen in the hedges, and we made blackberry jam. One tea time, we buttered bread, spread on jam, and then covered the jam with thick Cornish clotted cream. I had just cut through these layers, when I happened to glance down, and cried out, "This is it! This is it! The slipware!" The knife had left

53

patterns like those on slipware through the layers of cream, jam, and butter. I looked at Leach, and he nodded. We rushed to the workshop, leaving the sandwiches uneaten, and tried our new discovery. Never mind tea time. It worked, beautifully! The mysteries of slipware decoration were solved at one try! How interesting that a technique should be discovered in such a natural way. From food to potting. We were able to apply what we saw directly to our problem. It was a good feeling.

At about the same time, a young man by the name of Adams at a pottery in Poole in southern England also discovered the same method. He sent us a letter explaining his discovery, and we exchanged letters expressing our strong ambition to revive and preserve the British methods.

In addition to the slipware dishes owned by the neighbour, we heard of another one, which someone reported to be in an antique shop in Plymouth. The price, he said, was one pound. Leach sent a postal order for it. For a long time it did not come. I thought there must have been some mistake and sent a registered letter. But finally it arrived. And a very fine dish it was. Yellow with black lines —very quiet, almost Sung in feeling. We were all overjoyed by this acquisition. I remember taking a photograph at that time with Mr. Matsubayashi from Uji, who was there. A quiet man and very interesting. All of us holding this plate. As far as I am concerned, even if I lost every piece that I own in my household, this is the one that I would like to keep most. A crack formed later, but I have repaired it.

Leach:

Hamada even as a young man was a friendly person. He was lovely with our children and he made a friend of an old fisherman down at the harbour front— Old Basset. This man had many sons, some with boats of their own. He was the grandfather of a whole tribe. He and Hamada struck up a warm friendship, which led to him often coming three-quarters of a mile up the Stennack to the pottery carrying a crab or lobster. He would arrive at about half past four, when we expected to finish work at five, and he would put it down saying, "You can use that", or grunting some such word or two. He would sit in silence, watching Hamada finish his day's work on the wheel, not interfering, just watching as one fisherman would watch another on a boat, noting with almost invisible approval what he knew to be good from his own craft sense. Then sometimes he would join us in a meal before the fire-place in the corner of the room. There we burned logs, and the table in front of it was where we would eat. Gradually he emerged from his silence, and later in the evening he would begin to express ideas that were remarkably intelligent. But his intelligence was of a man who had learned his wisdom from a craft of life. The friendship lasted all the time that Hamada was here and even after he had gone. When Basset died, I went to his funeral, partly for Hamada's sake but also for my own.

November 20th, 1922

Dear Leach,

Very glad to get your letter, hearing you have sold some etchings and many people took the exhibition seriously. I was rather anxious you were too busy to arrange pots.

We have started raku and hope to finish firing about one hundred pots by the end of next week. Mr. Nance came last Saturday with Dicon and will come Friday again to paint some.

I went herring-catching one night with Old Basset. Over 5,000 herring a net. Watching their start from the quay and their quiet work in the dark sea impressed me very much. They still have the right mind and true love for their fatal hard work. Some of them, with straight-looking eyes and heavy voices, in their old costume, were splendid.

Basset brought some ashes from the kippering place. I noticed in washing they contained a considerable amount of sand, but would do for some glazes, like tenmoku, anyhow. I will send some to Murray to ask for testing at his convenience, and if he thinks it useful to him, we will get more.

Mrs. Mairet sent you a notice of her show, which I enclose herewith. She says she now "is selling" without a word of show or exhibition. I feel embarrassed for my idea of using photographs in ours. I wish I could reproduce even such an announcement as hers in some Japanese magazine. Certainly Tomi would like the notice. If you go to her show and find some cloth to fit me for a suit ($6\frac{1}{2}$ yds. × 27 in.) and an overcoat, please get them for me.

You wrote in your letter Tomi has just come back from Korea with Yanagi in great excitement. I can imagine him in Korea, excited by not only pottery and other arts, but Korean life.

I think there are hardly any pots in the world through which a people's life breathes as directly as Korean ones, especially Yi dynasty wares. Between pots and life, Japanese ones have "taste", Toft wares have "enjoyment", even the Sung pots have "beauty", and so on. But the Yi dynasty pots have nothing in between; peoples' lives are directly behind the pots. (I think you understand what I mean in my curious expression. Of course, I am not comparing their greatness at all.)

Since I saw the illustrations in *Shirakaba* [magazine], my love of Yi wares has reawakened strongly, and I feel so happy to think of them during my evening walk. I doubt strongly if playful lovers of Eastern things or collectors who simply follow fashion after fashion could really appreciate Yi pots, where they would fail to find any curious shapes, beautiful patterns, and richness of glazes.

Give my kindest regards to Murray.

More luck on your exhibition.

Yours,

S. Hamada.

P.S.   If you get a chance to pass by Paterson and John Sparks, will you be so good as to call and ask them the possibility of my show sometime next spring?

Leach:
I thought, and still do, that Hamada's early training in meditation, even though it was for only one hour a day, affected the whole of his life. It put first things first, the inner directing the outer. So although he may have been much more silent in those early years, that silence was not the silence of wilful aloneness but of a thinking man considering life more deeply than the average—hence his friendship with Old Basset, hence his love of the children and their love for him, hence the growing number of friends all through his life.

Hamada:
I am still delighted with the memory of Mrs. Podmore. She was so excited over what we were doing. She would come every day to see the progress of the work, driving in a horse cart, two huge wheels and a buggy. She was like a little chirping bird.

Leach:
She was called Dreolin, which is Irish for "wren", and there she was living in St. Ives, old, with very white hair and an imaginative mind, a friend of all the Irish poets. We both liked her immensely and learned so much from her.

Hamada:
She would come in such great excitement and haste that even the beautiful shawls she wore would be trailing behind her and almost falling off. She wore hand-woven dresses by Mrs. Mairet. We would be invited to her teas at her home close by, and we used to spend evenings with her. She had no pictures on the walls; instead she had her own clothes, made by Mrs. Mairet, hanging on the wall.

Leach:
Mrs. Mairet, Dreolin Podmore, and Edward Johnston—three people who stirred our sense of truth and imagination, who taught us how to be friends in many ways.

Hamada:
Perhaps my first real English tea party was at Mrs. Podmore's. Mr. Nance was there; she thought we would make good company. At this gathering, I thought, "Ah, this is the way to have a tea party; this is the real English tea." It was out of sincerity of heart, it was not formal, it was a right kind of cordiality. Mrs. Podmore was the one who showed Leach the mermaid carved on the old pew in the church at Zennor, near St. Ives.
Then there were tinkers who went round repairing things—roaming and re-

pairing. They would buy old, empty bottles from people, wrap the neck with a twist of cotton string soaked in alcohol, burn it and thus cut off the neck of the bottle, and with tin cans, gallon cans, as shades, they would make lovely lamps. The light came from a candle in the bottle and shone through a pattern cut in the tin. At the top was a large flat ring so that one could hold it by one finger without getting burnt. Then they would go and sell the lamps. I still have one from that period. Very simple but very well made. I would like to decorate my new folkcraft museum with these.

With such friends around us we knew we were being welcomed and understood. It gave us ease of mind to carry on with what we were doing; it was our moral suport.

There was a family near St. Ives whose daughter graduated from university and then went to Switzerland and Italy to learn the art of cheese making. She married a tenant farmer, who had been educated in one of the local schools. Grig, their name was. Everybody was surprised at this marriage. They were so happy, and there was a wonderful barn he had made. They were living in this barn, and there were no drawings or paintings on the walls. A quilt spread on the bed was the highlight of the bedroom. In the kitchen there were very fine tiles on the wall, old-fashioned iron pots and pans, and they had slipware for dishes. They burned turf in a huge stone fire-place.

We were invited to a dinner there. The other guests included an architect, a painter, a writer, and other good friends in the neighbourhood. Her husband had very little schooling, just grade school, so he did not participate very much in the conversation, which had turned to the new station built in London, Charing Cross Station, where there were decorations by Mestrovic and Eric Gill. The works of about four artists were exhibited there. When the guests discussed whose work was better and so forth, there was no pleasure for the husband. I was very impressed with the wife, who was neither ashamed of him for not knowing much, nor did she try to shut him up when he said something. She just understood him and embraced him with great loving thoughts. The young wife modestly joined in the conversation and agreed with what her husband said—a very pleasant scene indeed. When the young wife talked, the husband kept quiet and ate the food. But when someone admired the butter served, the husband's eyes sparkled, and he began to explain how the butter was made. He proudly said that he regularly supplied the butter exclusively to a first-class hotel in London. When someone mentioned how tender the rabbit meat was in the pie, he came to life and began to describe how he caught the rabbit, why it was tender—the entire chase with his hunting dog jumping over fences and running across fields. If the rabbit is killed immediately, the flesh will be tender. Such knowledge he had. We were all extremely interested and suddenly learned to respect him for what he was. It was marvellous to see this happen.

The rabbit meat pie was simply delicious. The meat was stewed together with onions and potatoes and was placed in a slipware baking dish before getting too soft. Then the pie crust dough was unrolled over the dish. Holes were put

57

in the crust to allow steam to escape while baking. I realized then that the holes were made into the initials S H—my initials.

In the large granite fire-place a turf fire was burning on the stone hearth. The chimney rising up the wall was equally impressive. It was all extremely imposing. After the stone flooring of the hearth was heated by the burning turf, they pushed aside the turf and placed the slipware dish containing the pie directly on the hot granite. They then covered the dish with a large steel pot and covered this pot with the burning turf. Unpeeled potatoes had been placed around the dish to fill the space inside the iron pot. When the pie was cooked the potatoes were done too. The potatoes were served with plenty of home-made butter together with the rabbit pie.

It was quite a feast at the farmer's house. The people, the way the slipware was used, and the way the food was cooked still remain vividly in my memory.

Six years later, I visited St. Ives, and I had an impatient desire to see the Grig family. On my way, I met a sturdy young lady riding bareback. She was on her way to the blacksmith. I thought she came from the direction of the farmhouse, so I called and asked her. She said she came from the very house I was to visit and that she was living with the family to learn how to make butter. She also told me that the house no longer could accommodate all those who gathered there, and many were renting rooms in houses nearby. I pictured then how the family had flourished since my last visit there six years before.

The kitchen floor was tiled, and the wooden handle of the door was hand-made. The quilts on the bed were brilliant in the chalky bedroom. The students gathered at the house were having a party. They invited me in and served home-made cheese, Cornish clotted cream, and tea. When I was about to leave the house, accompanied to the door by the wife, I noticed an old stone mason silently chipping new concrete window frames. She told me she used concrete to fill in the frames to save time, instead of stones, to repair the mullion windows. Giving the concrete frames a finish like stone, she said, would make them blend with the house better.

Leach:

We thought that the place in England that had the greatest vitality of thought and action in craftsmanship was probably the small village of Ditchling, in Sussex, just north of the downs near the coast at Brighton. There lived the best English weaver—Ethel Mairet. Her first marriage was to the great Indian art critic Ananda Coomaraswami, with whom she spent four years in Ceylon. She came back still predominantly English in her character, and her influence in weaving was profound in this country and abroad. I stayed with her from time to time in later years. Hamada admired her and was also very much interested in Eric Gill, who lived in Ditchling—on the other side near the Common. He and Douglas Pepler, the printer, were leaders of a Roman Catholic group that lived in a compound of houses—The Gospels—with their own chapel. Their conviction, rather than producing a closed, narrow outlook, allowed an openness and natural acceptance of life. Gill once said to me, "I wonder what God felt like when he was cutting his toenails?" He, of course, is internationally famous as a typographer; he was the pupil of Edward Johnston. I think Hamada felt an affinity with this group; he recognized in them a quality or a form of life he had not seen before in English people.

Among that group down on the south coast, Edward Johnston stands out, to my view, as a most remarkable man; Hamada and Yanagi said that he was *the* most remarkable man they met in England. Why? Johnston's daughter, Priscilla, wrote a charming book about him, his wife, and family many years later. And she wrote back when I thanked her on receipt of the book, "What was it that made your Japanese friends say that he was a most remarkable man? For what purpose?" I told her, amongst other things, that he had no regard whatsoever for time, he was as timeless as an Oriental. She replied, "Of course, I should have known." This did not mean strictly to say that he had no regard for time, but he looked upon it as a secondary, extra fact of life, not to be obeyed slavishly. He was timeless. A perfectionist, he was a reviver of writing—not only for England but also for Europe. He was a half-hidden but penetrating influence. I have never met anyone who had been in his classes, which he sometimes gave in London, who ever forgot them.

Hamada:

When Leach and I visited Mrs. Mairet, the mother of English hand-weaving, in Ditchling, Sussex, she served us dinner using a complete set of slipware, which I have never forgotten. The dishes were products of Fishley, a potter who preserved the good traditions of England, the last one to do so. His slipware was often put on display in the market and sold there. The large and small pitchers, oval dishes, and green plates all went well with the large oak table. When you are invited to dinner by someone, you often notice, as a potter, that dishes of lower quality are used together with superior pieces. But Mrs. Mairet served food on the best dishes, a perfect score.

I have great admiration for Eric Gill. I admire his works as a sculptor, as a wood engraver, and a critic, but I have a greater admiration for him as a man who lived in his own way.

I recall that Leach and I first visited him after nightfall on the day following our visit to Mrs. Mairet in this remote village. It was in the autumn of 1921. As we opened the gate, we were surprised to see a cow coming towards us. Immediately the door of the house opened, and with the lamplight behind them, Mr. and Mrs. Gill and their lively children came out to greet us.

In the long and narrow dining room, which seemed to have been the kitchen of a farmhouse before, a big marble fire-place made by Gill was set, with a fire burning bright. On the table were cold meat on pewter plates and bread on wooden plates. Gill used an ingenious pothook, which, as he explained, saved the trouble of picking up the kettle to pour hot water. It was really a pleasant and congenial dinner.

Mr. and Mrs. Gill gave their children an ordinary education. After that the eldest daughter went to Switzerland to learn about cheese, and the second eldest daughter was practising hand-weaving under Mrs. Mairet. In a tone of reticent warmth, Gill asked about Japan.

On the following morning, we saw Gill's studio, a printing workshop next to the studio, and the chapel, which housed an image of Christ made by Gill. In the studio I noticed that tools, chisels, and hammers were very neatly arranged and that the drawings done by the children on the white wall had been modestly erased, except the best pictures. Two years later I visited Gill again and then once more with Yanagi in 1929.

I was impressed by a sort of unity—not forced unity—wherever Gill settled down, in the house or studio. Mrs. Mairet's home also had unity, in the building, furniture, and fixtures, and even in the way of dining. What struck me there was a sense of warmth abundant enough to silence a critical view that she must have taken the trouble to create the unity. Comparison with Gill's place was interesting to me.

Gill and Mrs. Mairet had firm convictions and composure in their works and lives. Firm conviction can be attained with brain, but composure cannot be reached unless we have a good life to support it.

When I met Edward Johnston, he told this Japanese story he had heard about two frogs. One was going from Kyoto to Osaka, the other coming from Osaka to Kyoto. In between there was a mountain and they met at the top of this mountain. As we know, a frog's eyes are located at the top of his head, but when he stands up, he sees what is behind him. So when they met at the top of the mountain, the one that came from Kyoto was looking at Kyoto, and the one that came from Osaka was looking in the direction of Osaka. The one coming from Osaka said, "Well, if Kyoto looks like that, I might as well go back where I came from." And the one coming from Kyoto said, "If Osaka looks like that, I might as well go back to Kyoto." They did not see anything beyond what they came from. So they went back.

Johnston thought this was very refined humour, and he was very impressed with the Japanese for having created such a story. Johnston was a man who liked solitary walks. He had a ladder made that led up to his room, so that he could go out without being seen or accompanied. That he did not want to be questioned by his family, and also his like for stories such as the one mentioned, I thought reflected his character very well. He asked me to tell him more such stories; I did not realise how difficult it was to tell them well.

Leach:

One of our friends who got caught by the love of potting was an American scholar named Henry Bergen, who was very much devoted to Oriental arts, especially Japanese. He had a collection of *ukiyo-e* colour prints, sword guards, and so on. I have forgotten how he got in touch with us; I think he came to one of our exhibitions and started to talk to me. He and Hamada and I became very good friends, and he loved to come down from London to try and make pots. He had been trained in Germany in philosophy, and was rather precise and Germanic in his approach. He would not let himself go. I used to say, "Can't you let yourself go a little more freely, Bergen?" But it was no good, it was too late to make a change of that sort. He was really a student of Middle English. That study had increased his meticulousness, and yet he was a good tennis player and played at Wimbledon. Working clay is not like stroking a ball over a tennis net. He would come and help us fire the kiln, and when he had any spare money from his work on Middle English, he would come and spend a fortnight with us. What a good friend he was and how he stroked my first book, *A Potter's Book*, with a pen instead of a racket.

When we arrived in England, the movement started by William Morris represented by the English Arts and Crafts Society was in its old age. Neither of us really joined it. I was refused membership at my first attempt to join, although I was accepted later and have exhibited in its exhibitions from time to time. Neither Hamada nor I fully agreed with that approach to crafts, and Hamada never exhibited at the society's exhibitions. To both of us the movement contained something antipathetic and somewhat sentimental. However strong their reaction to the utter dominance of the machine over the hand, I think we both felt that the work done by many of the members was tinged with self-conscious efforts towards a medievalistic revival rather than the real thing—much in the same way as the Pre-Raphaelites stood in comparison to the artists of Italy prior to Raphael. There was an element of sophisticated imitation quite different from inevitable birth.

There were others, too—there was Ethel Mairet's younger brother, Fred Partridge, a nice woodworker on a small scale. There was my old etching master Sir Frank Brangwyn, who lived near Ethel Mairet and whom I visited once or twice, and whose wife was Japanese. It was a good place; Hamada loved it, and I think they loved and admired Hamada, and later, Yanagi. I think they felt in him that here was a person who was down to earth, and they appreciated the reward of being able to make exchanges in the language of craftsmanship between East and West.

Another man who during these three years became our friend was Staite Murray, the best-known potter in England. Murray met us in the Artificers' Guild at my very first show. He walked round a glass case, and I walked round a glass case, each eyeing the other and each wondering who the other man was. He was obviously engrossed with pottery. We broke the ice and began to talk, became friends; I used to stay with him in London, and he came to St. Ives. I remember he was trying to use my Japanese handwheel, which is turned by a stick catching a notch in the heavy wheel head. It had to be spun by that stick in the notch to obtain momentum enough for throwing. Learning the correct way to hold that stick and spin the wheel with minimal effort is not easy at first. I remember him sweating over the wheel, looking up with a red Scot's face, sweat dropping onto the pot below. And would he give in? No. That was not his character at all.

There were potters influenced by late, rather decadent Japanese Tea wares for ceremonial use, but the standard was not high, nor were the Japanese samples good, and the movement died out in the first decades of this century. Murray

61

was thirsty to know about Oriental methods and had found his way to making stoneware. Hamada was delighted; he never had any idea of secrecy about pottery techniques and he answered all Murray's questions freely. Staite Murray was the first in England to gather a following of people who perceived that a potter could be an artist and that good pottery should be evaluated as an art and paid for accordingly. There was a time when he charged one hundred and fifty guineas for his most expensive pot, which was called "Ra". He had exhibitions also at the Paterson Gallery in Bond Street. I do not know how much Hamada gained from Murray, except in a general way in estimating the background of crafts in England in comparison with Japan. Certainly Murray was a force in the land, he was a leader. Here was a potter asking to be recognized as an artist—one of the manifestations of the development in this country of a new aesthetic that had been evolving since the latter years of the nineteenth century.

Hamada:

Sometime in 1921, Leach and I went to the Artificers' Guild, where we met Staite Murray for the first time. Murray's bowls did not have any footrings, which I found rather strange, and I asked him the reason. Murray's reply was that all the bowls he had hitherto seen had been in museums on shelves, and he could not see the feet. When Staite Murray came to St. Ives, I showed him how to make footrings.

Henry Bergen became friends with us and came down to St. Ives—he may have overlapped with Staite Murray. Murray was as obstinate as any Scot can be; he would not give in, he got as red as a turkey-cock and nearly bit his pipe in two, but he went on throwing; and so did Bergen go on scratching raku or something of that kind with a persistence of a good student of philosophy (he was trained at Heidelberg). Though they were quite different in character, there was a certain obstinacy in both, interesting to compare. Literature was Bergen's field, and he had no serious intention of becoming a potter. But Staite Murray was the most promising potter in England at that time. More than promising: he started something that extended the interest of London collectors of old Chinese classic pots and so on, first to the pots that he made, and then to Leach's and my work when we came on the scene as friendly rivals, so to speak. There was a certain tension, which, though unwanted, developed between Murray and Leach. Murray was the first individual potter to exhibit with the avant-garde painters and sculptors. He was exhibiting and selling pots and later belonged to the group that Ben Nicholson started. From that point of view, he was the first English artist-craftsman identifying himself with the fine arts movement.

Leach:

At this point one comes to the advent of my first student, Michael Cardew. This young man was as handsome as a Greek god, with forehead and nose all in a straight line, vivid eyes, golden curly hair, and a good strong jaw. He had just taken his degree at Oxford, was expecting a literary career, and had come down to see an aunt in Truro. Having heard of the existence of a pottery down at St. Ives, he came on to see what it was like. He peered in anxiously, "Can I come in? Are you potting?" He said he had done some himself in North Devon during his holidays, working with the last of the English traditional country potters, Edwin Fishley. At the beginning of his third year at Oxford he got a good dressing down—because of his consuming interest in pottery—from an uncle who was a don, so he completed his four years. Thus he attained to some extent an orderly mind and a good style of writing English, whilst preserving more primitive instincts and intuitions.

Within a quarter of an hour of his arrival he had asked whether he could come and join in our life. Since writing these lines I have read his own written account of this episode; my memory, although seemingly definite, is nevertheless wrong. I was not present, apparently, when he arrived, and it was George Dunn who met him, saying that I had returned home but that Shōji Hamada was there; would he like to see him? He did, and Hamada was sufficiently impressed to walk him across the lanes and fields all the way over to the Count House, where I lived.

In due course I went to see his father up in North Devon near Fremington; he did not object to Michael's working with me. We went up on my first motorbike and side-car. I remember clearly how it took us two days and how frequently something or other went wrong with that Martinside machine.

Cardew and his brothers were all rather unconventional. They had an invalid mother and grew up rough and ready, loving the country, fishing, and classical music. Everybody in the family seemed to play some musical instrument. Michael came to St. Ives and joined in rather towards the end of Hamada's time here; I think we three spent six weeks or so together and met again in London during Hamada's exhibition. Often in the evenings we would sit at the table examining shards that had been ploughed up from the field opposite.

Cardew left, to our sorrow, after about a year and a half, but he took with him our combined discoveries concerning eighteenth-century slipware to Winchcombe in Gloucestershire, where he lived for many years and made the best lead-glazed slipware seen in England since the eighteenth century. After a long sojourn in Nigeria after World War II, where he was the British Pottery Officer in the civil service, he returned to his native Cornwall, where he still is today at Wenford Bridge. But now he has left slipware behind him and has gone on to stoneware. Nevertheless he started a wave, and it went East and West, resuscitating, starting fresh combinations, seed falling on good or indifferent soil or on no soil at all.

Michael Cardew:
This is one of my life regrets. I went there, I think it was late July, as soon as I was through with Oxford. Hamada was there. He was working for a show. I suspect I was there for a month, and it must have been late August when a friend invited me on a Mediterranean trip, and I was not going to miss that. I was away for eight weeks—a critical eight weeks. I got back at the beginning of

63

November, and by that time Hamada was in London having his show. That is the last I saw of him. Bernard said to me, "Well, what're you doing here in London?" and then I went back to St. Ives and got on with some work.

Yet Hamada's influence on me was definite. He made the most lovely raku out of red clay. Well, it was slipware, but it was fired with raku glaze. Red clay dipped in white. Sgraffito decoration. Dashes of copper green. Lovely stuff.

Hamada's pots said much to me. That was chiefly because Hamada was a natural potter. There are natural potters and there are potters who are moved more by conviction. The other thing was that, at that time, Hamada was extremely excited by Chinese peasant ware and by English peasant ware. When I first saw the Chinese peasant ware with sgraffito on red clay from Hupei Province, I said that's where Hamada got it from. Of course he would be the first one to say so. All good potters start by literally copying very often. I was copying Fishley's pitchers—not that I'm a good potter. You do copy. You really really want to be in it. And you suddenly wake up and find that you are something else. The effort of copying has really set you off creating, but you do not know it. Creation is unconscious.

Hamada was a magic man. I first saw his pots rather than getting to know the man. Hamada's work was at its peak at the end of three years in St. Ives. But nobody could help getting to know him. I've always felt that Hamada was a friend because I admired his pots so much. And, of course, I saw much of him when he came back in 1929.

Leach:

This was a time of the first students, and of friends who were prepared to come and give a helping hand when we were hard up for labour during long night hours of firing kilns. These firings were mainly high temperature and lasted anything up to thirty-six hours in those days. We have gradually reduced the time to about twenty hours today.

Who else was there? After Michael Cardew came Katherine Pleydell-Bouverie, who is still making pots—an old lady now and a very lovely person. Her contribution has been important mainly in the use of somewhat matt-surfaced glazes in the composition of which the Oriental habit of using various wood ashes is normal. I do not know anybody who has looked into this procedure as thoroughly as she did. Then came Norah Braden and then others, some of whom did very good work, some with great promise that was not fulfilled.

Hamada was an incomparable companion. We never irritated each other, or if I did irritate him, he never showed it. He was very thoughtful, not as talkative as he has become today by any manner of means, but rather silent. Not exactly shy, but on the week-ends he would go off if the weather was fine and lie on heather near the sea edge or on a cliff and be alone with himself, thinking, not meditating, contemplating perhaps—a kind of meditation. This was derived from a training he had when he was boy of about fourteen, when his health caused anxiety. His family feared consumption, his stomach was out of order, and his teeth were decaying. One day his father said to him, "Now, lad, you come with me every morning, and we'll go to a certain house on my way to business and spend an hour there together in silence." They went, and Hamada described the process of sitting in a room in hot weather fully clothed and in winter weather naked to the waist. They sat with their legs crossed in the accustomed position of meditation. They were instructed to hold in their minds a single Chinese character that denotes the navel, which, in the Orient, is regarded as the very centre of the human system. It is not just the physiological meaning of the word but its inner content, its inside-outness. The navel was the centre of himself and, for the moment, of the universe. It was the umbilical cord between himself and all things.

They held that thought as if it was a gift, something precious held in their hands, and kept their minds from wandering off in various directions, not thinking how big it was or anything rationalistic about it, but of the centre of oneself, one's being, a human being in nature amongst other human beings. I asked him the result, and he said that he got better and better. I asked if there was nothing else, and he said that he was told to sit with an upright spine, to breathe deeply, filling the upper part of the lungs full, holding the breath, expelling it through the mouth by contracting the stomach muscles, pausing again, refilling, and so forth in a very slow manner. And the effect on others? There were a few women there, he said. One old woman, quite uneducated, was asked by one of the party at the end of a year, "How big did you see the character for 'navel' in your mind's eye?" "In the first month," she said, "I saw it as big as it is written on the page, the second month I saw it as big as the page, and the third month as big as the room." "And then?" "Then I saw it as big as the universe." This was the thing that turned Hamada from a rather weak boy into a healthy youth, and that gain he has retained all his life.

I do not pretend to explain this, but it is a fact. He used that kind of quiet approach; it appears in his own sense of rectitude, in his thoughtfulness, his inventiveness, his usefulness as a human being, in the further development of himself. At week-ends he would go off to the heath or the cliff-tops to be alone and come back and start every week quite clear in mind, quite . . . what shall I call it, the *whole* man facing events day by day, dealing with each before the next demand arose. I think this is significant in the life of Hamada because, of all men I have ever known, I have not met another whom I never saw angry. I think this was one of the things that came out of that one single year of one hour a day in his formative beginnings of mature life. Anyhow, I think it helped enormously to work beside such a man. He said, too, that he was always thankful that he came with us to St. Ives instead of going to China.

Hamada:
I often went off to the cliffs. One day I was lying on a slab of stone on the cliff for a long time. Unknown to me a cuckoo came near. I never expected a cuckoo, a wild one, to come so close to man, almost to my head. Suddenly the bird cried out "Cuckoo". I was startled—and then I *knew*. I was twenty-seven years old when that happened. "Ah," I thought, "I am here. I know it." Any explana-

tion added is nothing more than a betrayal of that experience. This is the central core of this book. From there begins my real life.

During those days we were so poor I had no chance to go off and see anything of England, and Leach kept apologizing for this. But apology was not necessary, because from that small place I was able to see out into the world. I think my experience in St. Ives was invaluable. No matter where you are, experience must come to you. It did not have to be St. Ives, but to know that I was on the other side of the earth had a special meaning.

Leach:

In the autumn of 1923, Hamada's last year, suddenly one day we heard the news of a terrible earthquake that had affected the area of Tokyo and Yokohama. It may be forgotten by most people how serious it was. Tokyo, one of the biggest cities in the world, had hardly a building left standing. The wonder was that the hotel designed by the American architect Frank Lloyd Wright did not fall. It was a frightful disaster; the aftershocks went on for three days. I have a book devoted to photographs of it—the railway lines were like snakes and there were great cracks across roads. There is a saying in Japan, "When the big earthquake comes, run for the bamboos." The roots of the bamboo are fibrous and so tightly bound one to another that a piece of land on which bamboo grows may form a raft in itself and cover any crack that may open up below.

Hamada's people were all in Tokyo, and for three months we could get no news of them, nor of those people who belonged to Matsubayashi, who was still here. Of course we were in touch with the Japanese Embassy, but it was a most gruelling time for them. Hamada did not know if his father was alive. He had an ink factory close to the Sumida River, which runs through Tokyo. His father told his crew of thirty or more who were working there to put on their footwear—Japanese in warm weather will go barefoot, and this is impossible when fires throw showers of burning embers. Hamada's father and family made their way to the one bridge across the river that did not fall, and there they escaped with their lives. But we had to wait three months before we heard anything. There was an uncle of his and his family on the other side of the Sumida River. Embers were carried right over it, though it is as wide as the Thames. Some people escaped by standing up to their necks in the river with a sodden cushion over their heads. It was a truly major earthquake—over a hundred thousand people killed, and a huge amount was destroyed and had to be rebuilt. The new Tokyo was utterly changed, but, in fact, every time I have gone there during the last half-century, the changes (not necessarily by earthquake) have been so great as to make streets unrecognizable.

Hamada had his last show at 5 Old Bond Street, and it was a great success. It made an impression in England that has lasted over the years.

About the time of this last show, before Hamada left for Japan, we received an invitation to dinner from Mr. Eumorfopoulos. His house faced the Thames, between the Tate Gallery and the Chelsea Reach. When we arrived, he invited us to come into an anteroom, where he had a collection of contemporary sculpture. There for the first time we saw the work of the Croatian sculptor Mestrovic and were much moved by it. After the meal he took us around his great collection and allowed us to handle his pots, which was a real pleasure. For one thing, we could turn the pots upside down and see how they were finished and see what the individual touch of a maker was like where the clay was exposed. His last remark shows the man's generosity. He said, "When you have a promising student I would gladly show my collection to him myself." He was a very quiet man, short of build, and with innate modesty and love for art. Once he came to my house in St. Ives and saw my greatest treasure—a fluted Tz'u-chou bowl of the twelfth century, which he admired, then paused, and said, looking at me, "Would you care to part with that?" I replied that I could not, for it was a gift of my Japanese friends on my return to England. He accepted my refusal without demur, but I sensed he would have paid anything for that pot, which is the finest of its kind I have ever seen.

Hamada:

Three years had passed, and we wanted to do something to show the result of those years of effort. I personally opened my first exhibition in London in the spring of 1923, and it was a great success. Leach also had one there later. I had gone into this very quiet gallery, called the Paterson Gallery, and sitting there was a fine old man. I was impressed with him, so I approached him saying that I wanted to exhibit there. He replied that it was a very rare thing to have a pottery exhibition, but since it was a very interesting proposal, he would take it on, and so he did. That was the owner, Mr. Paterson.

7th April, 1923

Dear Sir,

I am in receipt of your favour of the 5th inst. Your case of pottery arrived yesterday evening. Do you not think you are driving it very close if you only arrive in town on the 12th as it only leaves a day and a half to arrange the Exhibition seeing that it is advertised to open on the 16th. The Gallery and cases will be ready by Tuesday next. The Bill should be upright, 19×31 in. I presume you do not intend to have a printed catalogue as you say you have a list typed. We close the Gallery each day from 1 to 2 p.m. for luncheon, but if an Exhibitor wishes to open during that hour, *he* arranges to have someone here. My assistant will always be in attendance from 10:00 and from 2 to 4:00 and Saturdays 10 to 1.

Yours faithfully,

Wm. B. Paterson

Hamada:

I was very pleased with the way it went—men like Eumorfopoulos came the first day, and each bought something, not like Japan where they come in gangs.

67

These men bought thoughtfully. The exhibition sold very well—it was reported in the newspaper, the clipping was sent from one person to another in letters, telling each quietly that such an exhibition was being held, and slowly but surely the news spread and the whole show went quite well.

April 16th, 1923

Dear Leach,

Hamada's exhibition is going to be a great success. Many people came today and quite a number of pieces were sold. Winkworth (W) came early and bought some nice pots. It is by far the best lot H. has turned out, and the firing seems to have been all that could be desired —I imagine it is impossible to avoid a few underbaked pieces in a full kiln. The room looks very pretty with its dull mulberry velvet hangings, and the glass shelves are less disturbing than I thought they would be. The pottery shows up very well on them.

The new kaki [glaze] is very good indeed, and the fine vase dappled like the skin of an apple is a triumph. Altogether Hamada's work shows remarkable progress from all points of view, and especially the handling of the glazes and the development of his individuality. I should like to see a warmer yellow in the galena and wonder if a better colour could not be obtained by using white lead? The galena is so hard and brilliant, especially in combination with magnetic iron powder.

The body is very much improved, although still very hard—Cornish clay! If we do a Tenmoku kiln next summer, as I hope, we ought to have also a soft smooth body corresponding to the light-coloured Honan and Ting bodies. The quality of Tenmoku depends apparently more on the body than on the glaze, and the fine quality Ting and Honan bowls all have thin, light-coloured bodies. The Chien (Nogime [*sic*] and Yōhen) cups are glazed much thicker. I wonder if a little experimenting with the red body you used in early firings, with a little china clay or pipe clay and feldspar added, might not produce a smoother burning, softer body? The Ting body seemed hardly to change at all in the kiln. What I'd like to see is a soft body able to stand a high temperature, close-grained and light in colour. I fear it is a very difficult matter, and that it is a thing you want no less than I do and that the materials are not to be had.

Hamada spent Saturday afternoon and evening with me, and we had a good long talk, all about Zen and early pots and Japanese tea-ceremony pottery etc. On Wednesday I am going to Murray's. Murray was helping at the show today—a very fine man. Skinner was also there and Miss Horne and a friend. Martin Armstrong and Conrad Aiken and Mrs. Aiken were there when I came in. Nance and his friend Wills also came in just before I left about 4 P.M.

Sincerely yours,

Henry Bergen

April 17. Last night it suddenly dawned on me how to do plates of a certain sort—a flood of new ideas! At my age—nearly 50—one goes through various phases like a locomotive, quite apart from goodness or badness of work.

Hamada:

The fine old man in the gallery presented me with a Persian pot at the end as a gift, which I still prize. I made many friends at that show, and I experienced once again the quiet, conservative, thoughtful English tradition. The English are slow, but they are sure, and there is a certain precision about the way in which communication takes place. I realised that what I myself had mastered before was merely the decoration, the surface colouring, and that I had missed the more important heart of the English and their customs. Coming from the opposite side of the world in the East to the far West, I decided to do away with what I had hitherto learned and to start completely anew.

I thought then that a three-year stay in any country was required. I had come to be able to say "good morning" in the morning and "good night" at night in the most natural manner, and mean it, without any excitement or upheaval or emotion—this was the time when I really came to understand the English. The first year abroad everything is interesting, everything is new and exciting. The second year nothing is any good, nothing is of any value, nothing Western is exactly favourable or virtuous; you begin to negate what you have experienced. But the third year everything starts coming in without resistance. You just absorb what comes and goes without particular emotion, and this is when you begin to really understand the true nature of a country. I tell my children that it is always good to go perhaps just a little bit more than three years, but not to stay as much as four or five years. If you do that, you start taking on something of the other side without being exactly of the other side; you just become a "half-boiled egg", not quite settled in any country. One can remain Japanese and, having been somewhere for three years, can suck the juice from whatever experience one has and return and make it part of one's life, let it become absorbed in the very essence of one's life.

In September of the same year, the Great Kantō Earthquake shook Tokyo and the surrounding areas. I naturally worried about my family in Tokyo. It was reported in the newspapers that Enoshima, "a picturesque island", had disappeared. I could not believe this. We felt we had to do something, but all communication was cut off. There were no letters or cables for about three months.

Mr. Nance, in order to help the Japanese, wrote a play and had it performed. Money was collected from this and was sent to Japan somehow. It was reported in a Japanese paper that there was a contribution of seventy-seven pounds from Cornwall, gratefully received. Coming from such a remote part of the world as Cornwall, the Japanese knew immediately it must be Leach and Hamada at the other end who had been involved in it.

I do not remember reporting to any consulates or embassies in England, but

69

it was marvellous in those days that they knew where any of their citizens happened to be outside Japan. They had a record of me being in Cornwall. I had paid no attention to what was going on in Japan, but the Japanese were quite aware of what I was doing far away in England. It impressed and astonished me at the same time—there were all sorts of articles in the newspapers.

Finally letters began to arrive from Japan. Tomimoto wrote that things were in such a turmoil, surely there would be a revolution coming. Tomimoto was someone who would exaggerate quite a bit about things of that kind. "Indeed you are very fortunate to be in England," he would say. "Japan cannot go on this way, and when there is a revolution, I shall go to Shanghai." He said that when he got to Shanghai, he would try to make a living as a driver because he had a great interest in automobiles. And also watch repairing. "How I wish I could be with you." That is how upset Tomimoto was about Japan and its conditions. He found no time to make pots or fire his kiln.

Kawai, too, wrote to me, saying that the capital, Tokyo, was destroyed and how terribly worried he was because the balance of the whole country had been upset. Until the balance has been restored, I should not come back, he advised.

Tomimoto wrote to me in St. Ives at the time of my departure, telling me not to come back yet, not yet, not yet. But there was a change in Kawai's letters. This was because a Baron Iwasaki and Marquis Hosokawa apparently had come to Kawai and bought more than half his work. Because they had lost everything in the earthquake, they needed something and wanted to start a collection—they wanted to have something around them. They asked Kawai to let them buy whatever there was to be had, and both bought enough to have an exhibition. Kawai was astonished at this experience. He came to the conclusion that when Japanese are put into such situations of having nothing left, they will immediately begin again collecting more things. If they have this energy, everything will be all right. And Kawai advised me to rush home.

Finally I learned that my Tokyo home had burned down, but that my family was safe. I was the eldest son of the household, so I had to go back.

I had another exhibition in December of 1923, at Paterson's again. The whole exhibition was so successful that only three pieces remained. These were my favourite pieces, so I brought the three back with me to Japan. I believe one or two are in the Ōhara museum in Kurashiki, and I have the remaining pieces.

By the time I left St. Ives, the technical standards, using local materials, had reached the level we had planned, and we held exhibitions in London; Leach had been acknowledged as a potter, and Michael Cardew and other young people had come to him to study. Tsurunosuke Matsubayashi of the Asahi kiln of Uji, near Kyoto, stayed there for some time, gave very commendable technical service, and rebuilt the kiln.

January, 1924

Dear Matsubayashi and Leach,
In Naples, I received your letter dated the 11th. (Enclosed was a letter from Mrs. Horne.)

The ship's departure was earlier than expected. There was very little time in Sicily. I travelled here and there, stopping one or two nights. The day before yesterday I boarded the boat at Brindisi. The schedule is to arrive at Alexandria February 2, overland to Cairo, then to Port Said on February 4. I think I can meet the *Amazon Maru.*
. . . [miscellaneous impressions and discussion of schedule] . . .

I went through Rome, Naples, Pompeii, crossed over to Palermo, stopped at Girgenti [Agrigento], Catania, Syracuse, Taormina, etc., passed through the Straits of Messina, and returned to the mainland to Brindisi. Sicily was as interesting as I expected. There were numerous ruins from Greek, naturally, and Byzantine Norman times. The life of the people has much flavour of the Orient. It is rough but very interesting to me.

On the way back from Palermo I was invited into a house where they were making macaroni. While drinking the wine that was served, I watched the process. This resembled the primitive extrusion press-forming of tiles, but was on a much larger scale. The force of a rope wrapped around a post was used skilfully to mix and extrude the dough.

In Girgenti, more than the Greek ruins, I liked the town and its suburbs. I took out my camera and walked around with it for the first time. That evening an officer wearing a three-cornered hat and cape came with a translator to my hotel. But what was this? He had heard that I was carrying an unusual camera and had come with an interpreter to exchange camera talk. He had taken such trouble, but knew little about cameras and went away satisfied with having made my acquaintance. The hotel people, who did not know the details of the meeting (I heard later that he was rather a distinguished officer), seeing that he left satisfied, suddenly were terribly polite to me. The next day the owner and entire staff saw me off. I thought it was very funny.

Talking of officers, in Brindisi I encountered a very stupid one. When I was drawing a part of the church of Chiesa Santa Maria del Casale, he brusquely ordered me around and searched everything I was carrying, including my lunch. I had a thought. I opened my passport and showed him a letter of introduction written in French. He could read it. Then I opened my Baedeker guide-book, pointed to the English consulate, and insisted that he accompany me there. He seemed to lose heart somewhat, went as far as the entrance to the city, grumbled something, and went away. I had no desire or reason to go to the consulate. He had ordered me to tear up the sketch, so I put on this act for him. Ho, ho.

From Catania in Sicily, about three hours by train, I went to a town called Camutagoro [phon.; Caltagirone?], stayed one night, and saw the pottery there. This pottery was about the same level as those in Okinawa. Since I could not explain in Italian that I was a potter, following their suggestion, I made a piece on their wheel and showed them. They were surprised at Japanese skill.

Every day of this trip has been so interesting, there is not enough time remaining to satisfy me. Also, I have found a convenient ship from Italy to Port Said and luckily I have not been sick one day. I have been very busy, but the schedule has gone as planned. If something was to go wrong along the way or if there was no one like you to help me and I was to miss the ship in Port Said, I would be in a mess.

Since I realized this trip would be very busy, I decided that the best course of action always would be to limit any activity. It is unnecessary to pay attention to what are called famous places; rather, I should be prepared to receive with my own eyes completely, without tinted glasses, whatever appears in front of me. Thus, I try not to lose out to a busy schedule.

In the whole trip, French cooking, Byzantine art, Cimabue's frescoes, old craftsmanship, honest, hard-working, everyday life—generally I am satisfied with these impressions.

Ancient Greece (the beauty of early drapery on sculpture, the amphitheatre of Syracuse, the arrangement of the temple at Girgenti). Rome (here and there the lettering of ancient Rome—this I admired completely). Of course there are many good points about Renaissance things, but to me fine art and luxury are very remote. I have felt this keenly. Because the great works and masterpieces of which I had heard so much have almost no effect on me, I feel somehow desolate.

Now, because I have been leaning consistently towards one side, I am probably seeing things on the other side too casually. But, during my three years in England, my own perception unexpectedly developed far more than anticipated. I was not attracted by reputation. If I am now seeing only one side, and if this is inevitable for me, it can't be helped. I'm coming to feel that my life as a craftsman is increasingly rewarding in many ways; and my mind is becoming more and more single-tracked.

. . . [long section on advice to Matsubayashi] . . .

In my first letter I gave you various impressions of cooking, etc. in France. That alone is unfair. At least, I want to add English tea to that list. I have often spoken badly of English tea; now that I am away from England, it is the most nostalgic thing. How unexpected! Anyway, for either good or bad, the character of England is in her tea. Also the porridge, toast, bacon and eggs, and marmalade breakfast—after tea this comes second in nostalgia. I have become an Anglophile. Everyone lauds the wholesome life of the English gentlemen and ladies, but for me now, having travelled through France and Italy, the quiet, composed, richly beautiful English countryside I truly think is lovely simply as landscape. The English country churches also are splendid. I naturally agree with people who praise the beauty of Italy, but I wonder why so surprisingly few praise the English beauty. . . . [advice to M. to study England] . . . If the opportunity occurs, my desire to study England is very strong. Away from Japan, I began to understand my country; perhaps now I will gradually start to understand England.

Anyway, I was very happy quietly having many new experiences during those short three years. After banqueting fully on England, a nibble like this trip is significant; it is useful to enrich my sense of taste. Even so, how is it that travellers in Europe are satisfied to tour around and only nibble. Nibbles alone do not fill the stomach and in the long run do not digest into strength for work. Disregarding the people who travel for curiosity, amusement, duty, or exhibitionism, I feel strongly that young people should by all means find a place in one country and enter the life there.

Feb. 2—Because the ship stayed one day longer in Candia in Crete, I was delighted with the opportunity to see ruins dating from 3000 to 1500 B.C. (I liked them better than Pompeii) and the splendid collection of Cretan pottery in the museum. Some looked like handsome Korean designs. There were some designs that resembled my touch, but I was surprised to see so many that displayed Leach's character. If Leach can come here, he will never forget this museum.

The museum director asked me if I hadn't also come the day before. I then wrote my name, and he asked me if I was the brother of Professor Hamada of Kyoto University. Professor Hamada had stayed here two years previously. Japanese seem to get everywhere. After the English and Americans, it seems that the Japanese travel the most. In Florence, Rome, and Naples, I saw several Japanese every day.

I have tried to copy some of the Cretan designs.

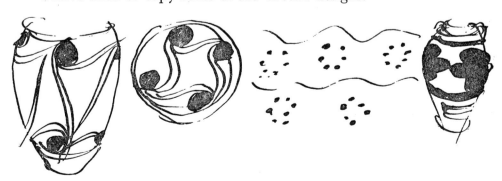

This design [right] is particularly like Leach.

These designs are beautifully drawn on large jars. Please try to envision them as drawn by brush.

There are much more elegant and amazingly skilful octopus designs—I can't copy them here.

I have brought this letter with me to Cairo and will continue writing here. I like this city very much. The Arab quarter is just like China. When I was staying at the Victoria Hotel, Professor Sentarō Sawamura of Kyoto University was there also. A number of years ago he was at the Ajanta Cave Temples for six-months' study, and before coming to Egypt he spent more than half a year travelling through China. He was a very fine companion for conversation. My appetite is still following an ordinary path—it is frightening.

The hotel is rather cheap, but everything in general is comparatively expensive. The hotel service is good and entirely in English style. Being at last in Cairo, I felt something lacking and looked for another place to stay, then moved to a Greek hotel. This is ridiculously cheap.

Until my ship leaves I want my stay in Cairo to be as long and as composed as possible. Of course I went to the pyramids sightseeing, but mostly I have gone to museums and to the Arab quarter. The blacksmith and medicine shop—in everything one can see the people's work and life. It is extremely interesting.

In old Cairo I saw a pottery village. Nearby there was an archaeological excavation. Persian pottery and Chinese celadon shards, etc. were being unearthed. It is said that Persian pottery production flourished even here; within a two- or three-mile square there are numerous shards. A guard came to reprimand me, but I showed him my passport. He thought it was a letter of permission, gave me a polite salute, and went his way. A passport is very convenient. Paying for an expensive revenue stamp has its benefits. I'm getting my "travel legs" and gradually getting plucky.

There are three museums; two of them are not famous—the Coptic Museum and the Musée Arabe. These two interest me. Coptic art is a relative of Byzantine. Not just the famous textiles, but everything is excellent. I like this art very much. In particular, there are numerous small crosses that are unforgettably good. Two students that I met eagerly questioned me about the Japanese position, culture, and relations with Korea. When I talked about Mr. Yanagi's museum, they were impressed.

The Coptic Museum is not governmental, but was built privately (an admirable person must be behind this project). The Musée Arab . . . is excellent (the collection of excavated shards is splendid). Today when I went there again, the curator kindly came to greet me and said, "I saw your name written in characters yesterday and understand you are Japanese. I am writing a book about Egyptian ceramics. May I ask you to help me with some of the Chinese shards here?" He was very pleased to hear that I was a potter and, more than treating me to cakes and tea, gave me some shards and invited me to dinner the next day. "Aren't we both Orientals? Please don't stand on ceremony."

Then we spoke of things I had long considered, of the bond shared by aware Orientals—that is, the lonely discomfort of Westerners vis-à-vis the Orient; the blind timidity of the ordinary Oriental people themselves.

I had been asked many times about our religion and about how we view Westerners. The two Egyptian youths at the museum even asked if I was Japanese and, if so, why I could speak English. More than the English position in Egypt, the Japanese position towards Korea is painful to me. Rather than transient politics, we then spoke of putting effort into art, which is lasting; the two replied that without gaining freedom they could not put effort into art.

At any rate, in this way my life in this city is more than what is seen by the simple traveller. Though I have stayed here only one week, yet somehow I already feel nostalgia for this place.

This has become a very long letter. After I started to write to you, my letter to Leach got included also. Say hello to Mrs. Leach and the children and to everyone at the pottery.

The boat leaves on the tenth, and I will go to Port Said on the ninth.

Shoji Hamada

Leach:

When Hamada departed, he left sore hearts behind, and the pottery seemed very empty without him. After he had gone, we really had to face a potter's life by ourselves. The public was not accustomed to the ideals that we were aiming at and had to be coaxed. It was a situation that we had to get accustomed to patiently, without giving way. There were at that time working in the pottery: Michael Cardew, Katherine Pleydell-Bouverie, George Dunn, Matsubayashi, and myself.

Those early years of the twenties were naturally hard times. We had used up the original borrowed capital in the purchase of land and building construction, and we had to make our own way forward. My inheritance was used up also, and sales were insufficient—bankruptcy was on the horizon. In this situation we had help from Japan: Japanese requests from Yanagi that I should send exhibitions periodically helped; we received the total receipts of the sales of those exhibitions in Tokyo! The Japanese from afar were helping to establish me, an Englishman, in my own country.

Hamada, when he got back to Japan, gradually became closer and closer to my old friend, Sōetsu Yanagi. This of course pleased me enormously. Kenkichi Tomimoto was in the offing and, in the early days of the movement in Japan, took part in the activities that were gradually becoming known as *mingei* (the word *mingei*, coined by Yanagi, means "art of the people", which corresponds to what we call folk art). This was happening late in the twenties in Japan.

Hamada:

I disembarked at Kobe, went directly to Kyoto to see Kawai, and stayed with him two months. Everyone thought that the reason why I had gone to Kyoto was because I had lost my family in the earthquake, but all were safe and well.

Kawai had lost all sense of direction. Because of the conditions in Japan he did not know what he wanted to do next and was very glad to have me with him. I arrived at night, and when Kawai opened the door he was quite startled to see me there. He responded with the intense feeling that he generally has about anything. The tears streamed down his face. At such moments he could hardly express himself. I was standing there holding only a single bundle of belongings. He thought I must be in terrible economic straits, and I had to tell him that all my belongings were coming after me. "Now everything is all right. We will always be together," he said. He was so glad to see me back. "Let us spend every day together; everything will be all right."

I reached Kawai's home about 8:00 or 9:00 in the evening, and we talked until 2:00 or 3:00 in the morning.

Then followed days of walking the streets. That is what I wanted to do most; I could not contain myself. I wanted to see Japan again.

We walked everywhere, visiting antique shops and pottery workshops. I liked to look into the high shelves in antique shops where the dust collected, or under the tables, and look for things that people had not paid much attention to for many years, to see what had been neglected. Usually the things kept in such places were what people had not bought, things left unsold. This was all very refreshing for me to see. For instance, an oil pot with a little handle is often used on a Buddhist altar for illumination. I felt that this would be perfect to drink coffee from. I looked at all these neglected articles in this way. There were so many things that could be adapted for use.

Then I went to the testing institute where I had worked to pay my respects and to report my return to Japan. As I came out, I passed a fish shop in the neighbourhood, where I saw, much to my surprise, a plate with the *uma-no-me*, the "horse-eye" design, on stoneware. "Why, this must be the Japanese counterpart of English slipware," I exclaimed. I jumped at this opportunity and entered the shop. "Won't you kindly sell me the dish that you're displaying your fish on?" The vendor said, "Well, my master isn't in right now; I'll sell you the fish but I don't know anything about selling you the plate." I went back that evening again to ask them for it, but the master replied, "Well, no, that's something that we prize very much in our household. We usually keep it high up on a shelf. Somebody brought it down by mistake." I said, "But you are the master; you can make the decision. Surely you can think of parting with it if you want to." We argued back and forth for quite a while. I did not give up. Finally the master said, "Well, suppose I give it to you for a hundred yen." Just to give an idea of how much ¥100 was worth in those days, the ship from Egypt to Japan cost ¥350. Even from London to Japan it was ¥450. He was going to charge me ¥100 for one horse-eye design plate. I argued, but the master of the fish shop refused to listen. I had to look elsewhere. I asked Kawai if he knew of such a plate anywhere that could be had, and Kawai said no, he had never seen one like that before. "Well, we must look for it together, perhaps in towns near Kyoto."

Kawai accompanied me everywhere I went. He seemed surprised at the things

77

I picked up to take a better look at or had an interest in. "What do you find so fascinating in such things?" he kept asking.

Leach had a Japanese plate—the kind used to catch oil in old Japanese lantern stands—with a landscape design, which decorated a shelf in the St. Ives workshop. We found one just like it. I asked the price of the plate, and the shop owner said, "One yen, twenty sen." I tried to get it down to eighty sen, but the man would not make it less than one yen twenty sen. Kawai, from the side, poked me and said, "You don't need that, it's of no value." I responded, "No, no. I lived with a plate like this for three years in Cornwall and I never got tired of it. I must have it." Kawai said, "I really don't understand." We went out of the shop and considered, but I could not forget it and went right back again and finally bought the plate for a compromise price of one yen. We took it home, to Kawai's place, and put it up. This time Kawai began to take more and more interest in it. At last he asked me to let him have it, but I said, "Wait, wait. While I'm with you here, we'll have the plate up to see, but let's go and look for some more." So the next day and in the days that followed we asked anyone we knew to search the city for more such lantern plates. In no time we had seventy or eighty.

In the meantime, Sōetsu Yanagi had also moved to Kyoto after the Great Kantō Earthquake. I thought it was a good chance to introduce Yanagi to Kawai, so I asked Yanagi to go to Kawai's with me. But Yanagi said that it was somewhat difficult to visit Kawai because of a criticism about Kawai's work that he had written on one occasion. Kawai, equally, felt rather reluctant to meet Yanagi.

Not too long before my return to Japan from England, Yanagi had organized an exhibition of Korean Yi dynasty ceramics at the Ruisseau Gallery in Kanda, Tokyo, sponsored by the magazine *Shirakaba*. It was, perhaps, the first Yi dynasty pottery exhibition ever to be held in Japan, and the magazine *Shirakaba* issued a special edition.

By coincidence, Kawai was holding his own exhibition at Takashimaya department store, and he happened to visit the Yi pottery exhibit. It was a great shock to Kawai, who had been concentrating on Chinese ceramics. Suddenly, in those Korean pots he saw something totally quiet—he had not encountered anything like it before. "It was a bit lonely in feeling," he said, "but so very peaceful and quiet." He had tried imitating Chinese techniques, but he could not outdo the Chinese pots; his work always fell short of what he was trying to emulate, and because of this he became louder and louder. Kawai probably knew this, and in this exhibition of Korean Yi pots he encountered something new that challenged him. "Yanagi is great," he thought. "This man Yanagi must be a great person." He saw Yanagi sitting on the other side of the exhibition room, but he could not bring himself to go up and say he was a potter; he was so ashamed of his own work. How could he call himself a potter at this point, he said to himself, how could he ever introduce himself as a potter to Yanagi? He hastily beat a retreat from the exhibition. On the tram back to his Takashimaya exhibition he forgot to get off at the proper stop and went beyond it—he was so depressed and ashamed. It was not a matter of simply learning something from the Yi pieces; Kawai was so shocked that he could not put his hand to anything for a while.

Just at the time when Kawai was getting a reputation from his two private exhibitions, aided by aristocratic sponsors and many others, the Yi exhibition was held. His dilemma could have been the reason why Kawai was anxious for my return.

When I came back from England, and he asked me immediately what kind of work I planned to do in the future, I realized he had been stripped clean of all the courage he had originally. I said I was not interested in making or creating something novel or refined or acceptable from the standpoint of the usual idea of beauty, but that I was aiming at making correct and healthy things, pottery that is practical and not forced, that responds to the nature of the materials. I did not want to make something outwardly beautiful, but to begin from the inside; health and correctness were more important to me. To do this I felt that I should seek a place in the countryside where the tradition of pottery was still alive.

In the meantime, the package I had sent from England containing ten slipware dishes and old German salt glaze bellarmine jugs arrived at Kawai's. Kawai admired the slipware, and he soon made pieces identical to the originals—so good that even professionals could not distinguish the difference.

I immediately informed Yanagi of the arrival of the slipware and invited him to come over. Yanagi, too, admired the slipware, which he saw for the first time. This meeting was a turning point and bound the three of us as lasting friends.

I told Kawai that I wanted to study what was traditional and alive, then go on to make something of my own, something new. Japan at that time was perhaps one of the few countries in which one could do this. In Europe, traditions were alive but so weak that one would be lost pursuing a single tradition—the old pots were better. In Japan one could learn from the past and then re-create one's own way from there; the tradition of domestic wares was still alive.

About sixty or seventy years ago, there was a tea-pot found everywhere in Tokyo. It was a teapot with a simple landscape design in black, brown, and green lines on a rather yellowish white clay. I frequently saw this tea-pot at lunch when tea was served, and it was also used for water at calligraphy classes at my primary school in Shiba. Later, after I took up pottery, I learned that the tea-pot was a product of Mashiko, in Tochigi Prefecture. My teacher, Hazan Itaya, identified the landscape on one side as Mt. Tsukuba, the one on the other side as Lake Kasumi-ga-ura, and the drawing on the lid as the famous plum blossoms of Mito.

His explanation greatly interested me and it led to my first visit to Mashiko in 1920, before my departure for England. In Mashiko, I was told that those pictures on the tea-pots were based on landscapes on tea-pots made at Shigaraki near Kyoto. Even by that time, pottery tea-pots had given way to enamelled kettles, and only elderly potters in one or two workshops were making such Mashiko pots.

According to the record, Mashiko ware was started in 1852 by Otsuka Keisaburō, a short history for a pottery village. Yet it started before the Meiji era, and the old traditions were still alive then. Mashiko ware must have received traditions as old as the kilns in Soma and, before that, Kyoto, from which the techniques came.

In 1923, Mashiko pottery was out of date; the ware was behind the needs of the times. This weakness is found in all folk ceramics that we consider to be good. Despite this failing, that old Mashiko kitchen ware was never bad. It is always a pleasure to recognize honest and good work, not just dismiss it as being out of date. Here was a traditional framework and clothing becoming to the framework, reflecting the climate and local culture of the place. In folkcraft, underlying, unseen factors as well as the obvious forms and patterns are decisive in evaluation. Such criteria are more important than whether something is old-fashioned or new.

In England I felt I learned the way the English appreciate their countryside. People there were not just escaping to the country; they had one leg in the city and went there any time they wanted or needed to and participated in the community, yet at the same time they truly and naturally enjoyed living in the country. I learned from this attitude and felt that I could apply it to Japanese living. I realised that I could have a home in the country and not be cut off from urban activities. Mashiko was certainly near enough to Tokyo for me to go to the city whenever I wanted. I thought it was an ideal place to be.

Already before departing from England I had decided that I could go to Mashiko to live. Seeing the life-style of Mrs. Ethel Mairet and Eric Gill confirmed my conviction about living in the country upon returning to Japan. I decided to move to Mashiko.

Kawai objected; he said, "What will you find there? You will be limited to making patterns in iron; there's no copper there, and you don't have any variety of pigment at all. You will surely get bored with being there." I retorted that a variety of pigments is not needed. This was a period when Kawai was becoming better known and was experimenting with many different effects. I insisted that I would be all right and so I went.

Mashiko was fine and the people quite nice, but they had a tendency towards stubbornness—they were not easily convinced. I did not mind what sort of place I was going to live in; I just needed a room to stay, however dark, to make my own simple meals, and to work. Finally, after much trouble, I found a place to work, but I was an object of suspicion. I was constantly confronted by the police or local authorities coming around to ask me questions. There was a kind of "communist" party active in Japan then called the Taishū-tō. The Mashiko people feared I might be a member—I was an outsider in a very conservative village.

Instead of the usual woven willow basket-cases that were used then to pack things for travel, I had a leather suitcase decorated with all kinds of labels that I had collected from various hotels and ship lines abroad. Surely, they thought, this man must have been doing something nefarious or suspicious. And for those local people I dressed rather peculiarly; I wore a sweater and corduroy trousers. They had never seen anything like this and feared I was very dangerous —maybe a spy—and needed watching. Even when I went visiting somewhere and stayed for any length of time, somebody would arrive on a bicycle and enquire after me, and sometimes someone of the household would go and inform the authorities of my presence in their home. Things continued like this during my first six years in Mashiko. I was simply charmed by their obstinacy. And I was surprised to find such a village, which retained all the old customs and habits despite the fact that it was so close to Tokyo.

Mashiko then had no artist-potters, only craftsmen making one or two household items each, such as cooking pots, grinding bowls, and tea-pots. I thought I could do good work in Mashiko.

In the early morning I would meet local potters, exchanging good morning greetings, and again in the evening I would exchange good nights. In between these two daily meetings I sometimes pictured to myself this man making fifty cooking pots today, that chap firing eighty grinding bowls, and I felt ashamed. I thought it was truly difficult for me to make my way in Mashiko.

Of all the families I got to know, I thought the Sakuma family was the finest. I thought that perhaps living with them and working with young Sakuma would be good. Sakuma himself was quite happy at this suggestion because he wanted to work with me, too, but it was his mother who objected. "All potters are very poor, and we cannot afford to have a guest in the house", she said. "If we have a guest, I must make special food for him, and if I make special food for the guest, all the children will want to have the same. It will just go from one thing to another, and we just can't afford it. I must refuse."

I begged her. "I will pay whatever you say, I will do as you want me to do, I will not ask for any extra luxury, and I will eat what you have on your plate". So it was agreed. It was July then, and I remember that we had egg-plant at every single meal; it was egg-plant in the *miso* soup and egg-plant pickles for breakfast. For lunch it was boiled egg-plant, and in the evening it was fried egg-plant. This lasted through August, perhaps to the middle of September— nothing but egg-plant from morning to night.

Sakuma was an extremely diligent and eager young man. During the day he worked hard making the water jars traditional to his family pottery. Then, at night, he wanted to "study" with me. We used a cheap, primitive oil lamp for light. There was no electricity then. In the late afternoon, Sakuma would clean the lamp chimney so that it would be clear for the evening's work. I would carry this lamp into the workshop and we would work—study—together until 10:00 P.M. Sakuma was my first real friend there, a valuable and fine person.

Then, when the cold winter set in, I thought of going to Okinawa. I had first visited Okinawa in 1918 with Kawai. In fact, before deciding on coming to Mashiko I had a choice of going to Okinawa or Mashiko. But the Okinawan life-style was too different from mine; I thought then it would be better to forget Okinawa for a while, until I felt the need to test myself. When and if I felt that my work was losing its life, I thought of going to Okinawa to rejuvenate and correct myself, to give myself another impetus. I considered going back and forth, spending the warmer days in Mashiko and going to Okinawa in winter. After all, I had no home at that time and could move easily.

It was the first December in Mashiko when Iseki came to me with talk of marriage, with an offer of introducing me to a young lady named Kazue.

The matchmaking took place in Tokyo. I wore the suit that Mrs. Mairet had given me. When she learned that I was to depart from England, she wanted to give me something, but she said that there was not enough time for her to weave anything before my departure. There was a suit of her husband's she had woven, and, although he had worn it, would I like to take it? I was very pleased; it was a brown suit with dots. Well, I had worn that suit many times over, which was obvious at a glance, but, nevertheless, I wore it to the match-making in Tokyo.

At this first meeting, the go-betweens were Iseki, of course, and Kazue's uncle, who was quite well known for his ability to analyze character from a person's calligraphy, in particular, the single horizontal brushstroke for "one". Iseki was also learned and quite well trained in seeing into a person's character. He stated, "If you think it's all right, why don't you make up your mind quickly and go through with the marriage." But Kazue was not quite sure yet; she was twenty or perhaps twenty-one; her mother, also, was not quite sure about the whole thing. But the father took one look at me and thought me a fitting son-in-law immediately. He said that if everything was satisfactory, we should go ahead with the marriage right away.

I had nothing; I had come back from England with nothing—I did not even have a home. They decided to have the wedding at Iseki's house, where I was staying while in Tokyo. The date decided on was December 21, the shortest day of the year, which was Iseki's choice. He said that if you are married on the shortest day, from the very next day your fortune will grow; this is the lowest point—you can only rise from there.

I decided not to have even a drop of alcohol at this wedding. Traditionally the bride and groom exchange three sips each of saké, but even that, I felt, was unnecessary at a wedding. But the middlemen, both great drinkers, grumbled, and as soon as the wedding was over, they both went off to drink at some local wine shops.

Also traditional is an exchange of dowries—the man's side gives the bride-to-be what is called *obidai*, "obi money", and the bride's side gives the groom a sum of money called *hakamadai*. The middlemen are kept busy serving as messengers between the two families, making and finalizing these arrangements. I did not want any of the traditional exchanges. It was quite enough to prepare the documents to make it official. Iseki objected, but I insisted on doing it my way.

For the banquet, I thought of this: let each person attending the wedding come with one dish—whatever dish of food was to his liking and whatever he knew how to make. For the plates I went to Chinatown in Yokohama, to a Chinese grocery store where there were many dishes to be had. These dishes could be used after our marriage as well. Kawai represented all my friends at the wedding. He brought a huge bowl filled with a Chinese leaf vegetable, not cut up but in its natural form, made into a soup.

The usual wedding traditions were disregarded: the wedding was not particularly auspicious; the food was very mixed because everyone brought whatever they pleased. All thought it was an overly casual way of approaching the whole thing. Fortunately, my future father-in-law trusted me. He told his daughter and wife to leave everything up to me and let me have my way.

The next thing was to find a home. Why waste time? The morning after the wedding, Kawai and I went to Mashiko on the early train to look for a house. I had my eye on one house, but, finally, could not buy it because of family trouble in that household. Not having succeeded in buying the house, we went off to Kyoto and stayed about a week with Kawai then departed for Okinawa, my second visit there. We stayed about three months, rather a long time, and I worked there and made some pots.

Upon coming back to Tokyo I wanted to have a small exhibition. Iseki had just built a new house, and it was in his house that we decided to have the exhibition. No price could be put on my pots yet because they really were not pots that were worthy of being sold. At first we left the prices up to the buyers, but customers began to say, "If these were ordinary things, we would know approximately what they should cost, but your work is unique; we don't have any idea what they are worth." So I was pressured into putting some kind of price on each item, but the prices were decided by my friends.

Ordinary tea-cups in those days sold at three yen apiece at the highest. So I priced my tea ceremony bowls at five yen apiece, and was laughed at by Kawai. He said teabowls should not be priced under ten yen. And I still feel embarrassed when I remember people asking me about my future and ideas regarding teabowls, because I had priced them higher than the other things. I felt that my responsibility was to produce the object, that was my world; from then on the buying and selling aspect of it was not my concern—that should be left to someone else.

Many of my friends came to see the exhibition, among them one young man of considerable wealth, Jirō Aoyama. I remember an encounter between Aoyama and Iseki. Aoyama wanted a pitcher with brown glaze and runs of black. It was made in Okinawa, I believe, and priced at twenty-five yen. He bargained and wanted it for twenty yen. Iseki, who had overheard the proceedings, said, "Now wait, Aoyama, you must not do this. You come from a very wealthy family and you're quite capable of paying the set price. You should buy the pot for that price. You think that getting it for five yen less is to your profit, but you started to bargain after the price was settled and you realized there was no going back on either side. That will never do; that kind of profit is no kind of profit at all. Now, what does Hamada say?" Iseki asked. And Aoyama replied, "Hamada says, 'Don't bother about bargaining; if you want to take it, take it for nothing'. "

"Then why don't you take it? Because if you do take it then you will always be indebted, and there will be no end to that feeling. There will be no finish to the deal. You think that if you pay a certain price, you just pay the money and

83

then you can forget about what comes before and after. That kind of psychology is a rich man's psychology and is not a good one at all. This is a bad habit that the rich have, and for such a young man as yourself, to start your life with such a way of thinking will never do," Iseki said.

This was on the first day of the exhibition. Even from the very first day, such incidents took place, and I found it a very fruitful beginning.

Postcard from Yanagi, Hamada, and Kawai:

Jan. 9, 1926

My dear Leach,

A happy New Year to you. Hamada, Kawai, and myself have been travelling in the province of Kishū, the southern country, not very far from Osaka. Yes, travelling, but rather hunting, not hares or birds but old curios. Thanks for Epstein, most vital and suggestive.   S. Y.

"horse-eye" design

One of the old dishes we got, made at Seto, about 50–60 years old. Popular kitchen ware of the time; painted in black; dia. 8 in. I am staying (making some blue-and-white) at Kyoto for a month. My letter will follow soon (sure).
Greetings to all.   S.H.

Many things to show you and to talk about.   K.K.

July 9, 1926

My dear Leach,

Mr. Taketoshi Iwai, a friend of ours (Kawai, Yanagi, and myself) who is a respectable journalist and an archaeologist, is going to England, and is quite keen for a visit to St. Ives with his friend Mr. Umehara, also an archaeologist, now in London. He made me write a letter to you at last! Mr. Iwai is very much interested in seeing you and your work, especially in talking with you in Japanese. He will tell you about our latest news (he came down to Mashiko yesterday).

They are also hoping to visit the stone circles and other interesting spots in Cornwall from an archaeological point of view. Please introduce them to Mr. Nance. They will stay at St. Ives for at least a week, I think. Will you kindly book rooms at a hotel for them.

Well, Leach, I am really ashamed for my "no letters" indeed, and have been very conscious of it, as I know how you once worried about Mr. Naka's "no letters". What news I have to tell you of these two years! I had better begin with a list.

	April	With the Kawai's in Kyoto; saw Yanagi and Tomi
	May–June	In Tokyo; found my family and relatives safe from the disaster, although some of their houses burned. Saw Umehara, Kono, Nagayo and Awashima (I am sorry to tell you he died this spring).
	July–Oct.	Experimental work at Mashiko
	Nov.	A visit to Kyoto
	Dec.	Marriage (with a "not intellectual" girl, in the traditional way. The matchmaker was Mr. Iseki and the banquet was cooked by my brothers and sisters in Japanese, Chinese, and European ways).
1925	Jan.–April	Worked in Okinawa. Okinawa is famous for red lacquer, once had beautiful techniques of vegetable dyeing, and still produces charming pots. The climate is semi-tropical. The people still speak old Japanese, for instance: *kōmi sōrē* (present Okinawa language) *kai sōrae* (old Japanese, now only alive in belles lettres) *katte kudasai* (modern Japanese; "please buy")
	May	In Tokyo. Managed your show at the Kyū-kyo-dō Gallery with Yanagi, K. Tanaka, Hasegawa, and Noshima and saw M. Tanaka, Takamura, Kenzan's daughter, and many other of your friends.
	June–Nov.	At Mashiko
	Dec.	My first show at the same gallery. I heard Kawasaki had kindly sent Bergen the translation of the criticism of my show by Yanagi. Two-thirds of the pieces sold (about 2500 yen; average price was just over 10 yen). Young people like good pots for use.
1926	Jan.–April	My first son Ryūji was born Jan. 8th. Made some blue-and-white, plain blue, and overglaze enamel at Kawai's pottery in Kyoto. Saw Tomi and Yanagi, and we often made excursions to nearby old towns to collect old and modern traditional crafts for the Japanese Folkcraft Museum which we are planning to build within a few years. You will have seen the prospectus of the plan through Yanagi or Kawasaki. We really wish

you were with us for such a chance.

May	A small show of my work at Mr. Iseki's new house near Tabata.

After the show, we settled here again and have just finished the first firing of this year at Mashiko. Tomorrow afternoon some chambers of the kiln will be opened.

(July 13th) The firing was successful. I am sending you some pieces of my recent work with four old Okinawan kimonos and some *yukata* cloth by Mr. Iwai and shall be very glad if you kindly send them as my presents to Bergen, Murray, Mrs. Mairet, Mrs. Horne, Mrs. Skinner, Mr. Paterson, Cardew, Dunn, and Basset at your convenience. I put their names on the objects, except the Okinawan kimonos, which please divide as you like between Bergen, Murray, Mrs. Mairet, and yourself. Several cups among the pots show different styles of my recent techniques. The blue cups and tea-pot with kaki glaze (glaze was sent from Mashiko) were fired in Kyoto, and the others all at Mashiko.

Mashiko is a quite comfortable village to live in, with paddies, fields, hills, and even small mountains. The people are rough, but simple and good. Several clays and important materials are produced in the village; especially the kaki glaze is splendid. It is made simply by grinding a certain soft stone which is commonly used for the local architecture, and only the addition of twenty percent ordinary ash glaze (*dobai*) to it gives a beautiful black.

The kilns are rather primitive. Neither saggers nor shelves are needed. The firing is partly reduced, neutral, and oxidized, and I can manage all sorts of things well, kaki, black, ame, white and green opaque, common transparent, and etc.

Clay balls, white silica powder, or *mominukabai* between them.

I find the Mashiko brushes which are used for painting the landscape pattern on Mashiko tea-pots very useful for my painting too. It can be made of dog's hair in the simplest way. It is not easy to manage painting at first—*gunya-gunya* [mushy and soft]—but you will soon be able to make thin or rich lines easily with it.

Try to make it, and tell Murray about the process.

In November I shall have my second show in Tokyo, and am going to spend the winter in Okinawa again (address your letters to Mashiko).

I saw some photos of your recent work (large dishes and others) in *The Studio*, and liked them very much. Do send them to Japan. We shall be glad to have a show for you anytime, although we are rather worried that the present bad circumstances in Japan might influence sales. I can see you are getting more English in your work, and I, too, am getting more and more Japanese. Since I returned home, I have felt the very intimate beauty of Japanese local traditional crafts as I expected. They seem to me much more natural and familiar than even Chinese and Korean things.

. . . [various personal news] . . .

With my best wishes to you and Mrs. Leach.

Yours ever,

S. Hamada

Leach:

It was during those years of the twenties that we in England were struggling to find the proper materials and to find sympathy with the public. It was difficult with the public. They had been conditioned to a set of values dating from the industrial revolution. The trouble was that man was getting separated from his natural background, the potter from his clay—clay had become refined into something called paste or slip and looked like tooth-paste. All the irregularity was going; the public wanted everything that the "court" wanted; rare, expensive, detailed, brightly coloured, extravagant, far away from the norm of life—the vices were evident in it, pride, envy, and all the rest. What our pottery brought from the East was very different. It was an appreciation of roughness of texture and of asymmetry. It was all very contrary to the expectations of Victoria's time and the Edwardian time after it.

It took us years to find collectors in London who understood Chinese pottery and thus were open to our efforts, but they did begin to appear. They were interested because they had begun to collect the newly excavated works of Sung dynasty China and Koryŏ dynasty Korea. They appreciated values other than the highly decorated, colourful qualities chosen by the courts of the world. They were the ones who came to our assistance when we were on the edge of bankruptcy once more. I sent out an appeal telling of our work and asking if they cared to take part in a proposal that we should give them the best pots of the year in return for any money they could put up for our continued existence. This carried us through another crisis. George Eumorfopoulos was the outstanding figure, but there were other collectors as well, some of whom had minds open to a new aesthetic.

As 1929 approached, we heard from Japan that Hamada and Yanagi were planning to come to England. That was the time in which they were laying the plans for the Japan Folkcraft Museum.

Hamada:

Leach had kept saying he regretted that during the three and one-half years of my stay in St. Ives there was so little opportunity for me to get around and see more of England. He felt badly about this. But from my point of view, the fact that I did stay in one place and did not move around helped me tremendously to know the country, to understand the situation, and to understand myself as well. No apologies are needed for that.

When I was back in Japan and told Kawai that I had stayed in St. Ives for three years and had hardly gone anywhere else, and that I was quite satisfied with this, Kawai responded that I was quite right to feel this way. There is a saying in Japan that the frog in the well does not know the great ocean—but Kawai's contribution is that the frog knows heaven.

There are many such aphorisms and poems by Kawai. One that I like very much is about a man entranced by the light of a fine full moon. "My hands see it, my body sees it, my eyes see it. Have I been fully bathed in this light? No, there is one place left". And he takes off his footgear and exposes the soles of his feet to the brilliance. There is a book of about one hundred such poems by Kawai, but if you see the poems written out in Kawai's hand, the calligraphy is so exaggerated that much of the fine sense of the poetry is lost. I have said as much to Kawai. If he could not exaggerate, he was not satisfied. From his point of view he was not exaggerating; this is the way he expressed his joy and exuberance.

Another aphorism of Kawai's is that on horseback one can view the scenery much better; if one climbs a tall tree, the vista widens further. His idea is that if you place yourself on a higher level, you need not envy other people, you do not have to be troubled by the smaller things of life. Whenever there was an occasion for a wedding gift, Kawai would write a poem, such as "The nightingale searches for his plum tree. The plum awaits the nightingale to come and perch".

Quite often when I travelled with Kawai I would be awakened in the middle of the night by Kawai crying, "I thought of it! I just found the right phrase", and I would be made to listen to his new verse. Kawai's writing is very good. Yet in ways he was over-emotional and therefore not strong, which surprises one. In the early days he was a very sharp person; on the surface he seemed to be very forceful, and most people thought that he had a very strong personality.

Kawai and I went one day to see Iseki. Iseki bowed very deeply and said, "Oh, you are the famous Kawai", and took a good look at his face and stated, "Mr. Kawai, you are a woman." This astounded me. I had always considered Kawai my elder brother, my example, who was so skilled at everything that I could not possibly be on the same level. Naturally, Kawai was even more taken aback and he could not reply. I had always thought that I could learn so much from Kawai, and as long as he was there I did not have to worry about my future very much. But I could not get this statement by Iseki out of my mind— that Kawai was a woman.

If one wishes to describe Kawai in terms of water, below a waterfall there is a deep pool; the depths of the pool are unmoving and silent. But Kawai is the water that spills out of this pool and splashes and sprays noisily into shallower places. In Japanese this is called *sessaragi*. The deep pool, the soundless water represents potential energy. The deeper the water, of course, the more silent it is. This is not for Kawai. He is not quite satisfied with this. He prefers the movements and dynamics of the splashing water; he likes to see the movement and have the movement be seen.

Yanagi, too, met Iseki and was told that he was extremely well balanced. But Yanagi was advised not to hurry, to take his time and do his work well because he was lacking in the "beastly" force, the animal power that enables one to sink his teeth into something and not let go.

Kawai made up very good titles for his books. One such title for a small pamphlet is *Tōgi Shimatsu*. *Tō* means pottery, *gi* means technique, and *shimatsu* means being able to complete something, to have everything finished. Kawai was extremely good with such expressions, and of all the book titles he created I think this one is the best. But, at the same time, the fact that it impressed me so much when I first saw it made me hesitate; the fact that it was so clever is what caught me. I thought, "Anything that clever cannot be right." After all, when everything is arranged and complete there is nothing more to be said.

Kawai got so caught up that he almost hypnotized himself into thinking that he had completed everything. After all we cannot really complete anything in our lives—that is not a reality. But with myself . . . not complete, negating, unfinished. Perhaps the negative and positive are not different. If one says "finished", there is no life there anymore, but if one says "unfinished", life continues, movement goes on. I was going to write a piece to match Kawai's, but because my work is always unfinished, I still have not written it. That is, after all, the meaning of unfinished. When something is unfinished, it is finished.

Tomimoto had written on the wall in his home, for his family and everyone to see, a motto to the effect that the Japanese have no concept of fifteen minutes. He explained that the whole Japanese life-style was not attuned to quarters of an hour; there are hourly concepts, but nothing less. This, he said, he learned in England. The Japanese indeed have very fine watches, but they do not really use watches in the sense that the Westerner does—the Japanese time sense is different. Tomimoto felt that was a very bad thing and he wanted to teach his two daughters and his wife, saying, "If we stay in Japan, we will never learn this, so we must go to England. And in order to go to England we must save money and the whole family must become aware that they are saving money towards a trip to England."

When I went to visit him and saw the motto, I got this explanation. But, after all, they did not get to England, although the trip was a great aim of Tomimoto's. Just by having written the motto he had in a sense made that thought complete. I also learned a great deal from Tomimoto.

In Tomimoto's case, it was with his whole body that he was able to make this complete. In the case of Kawai, he made many statements about completeness, but in actuality he did not complete anything, so his mind and body were not one. This is so obviously clear in his work; in every pot he made this is exposed.

Kawai and I frequently visited the Yanagi's, and each time Mrs. Yanagi prepared exquisite and delicious food, served in highly treasured dishes. From her we learned much.

Upon entering Yanagi's house, wherever he lived, the house was invariably filled with the fragrant and exclusive atmosphere of him—in the study, living room, kitchen, and even in the dishes used to serve food to the cats and dogs.

The three of us frequently made trips, visiting antique and second-hand shops in the countryside and even in Korea and Manchuria, collecting folkcrafts.

Our journey to north-central Japan was most impressive. In Kanazawa, with the nearest second-hand shop from the station as our base, we made a round of over 170 second-hand shops in the city and had the goods we bought delivered to the first shop. By the time we were to board the train in the evening, we had to rent a cart to carry the goods to the station.

And in the spring of 1926, the three of us made an unforgettable journey. We travelled down the paths of Wakayama Prefecture exactly as did Priest Mokujiki in the sixteenth century, according to his diary.

Since I had never climbed Mt. Kōya, Yanagi guided us up the snowy ascent to the top. We stayed overnight in a room of the West Zen Hall in the temple complex and continued the discussions we had started during our climb. There Yanagi wrote the first line of the prospectus of establishing the Japan Folkcraft Museum, beginning with the words *Toki michite*, "The time is ripe . . ."

Rousing Kawai, who was dozing, we then talked throughout the night, discussing what concrete steps we should take to realize our plans of establishing the museum. We mapped out a programme to make collecting tours in the neighbouring prefectures, distant districts, etc. At first we called the items we were collecting *getemono* (to the Japanese this word meant cheap, rough things), by which we meant craft objects of popular use, in contrast to *jōtemono*—refined, decorated things. But the word *getemono* was rather commonplace, and we were afraid that the word might be misconstrued and misused. So sometime prior to our visit to Mt. Kōya, Yanagi, Kawai, and I had decided to coin a word. After heated discussions, we settled on *mingei* by shortening the term *minshū no kōgei*, "folk handcrafts". This was decided while we were travelling in a train.

Since the word *mingei* was new in those days, we had to explain what it meant at every lecture. It was also the time when mingei products, old and new, were truly abundant.

In October of 1936, we finally established the Nippon Mingei-kan (Japan Folkcraft Museum).

Today, the word *mingei* is part of the Japanese vocabulary, but its true meaning is as little understood as when we first coined the term. It is also true that the number of good mingei objects, both old and new, have decreased drastically. There are many souvenir shops with signboards advertising "mingei" items, but most of these shops sell nothing of the sort.

Folkcrafts have always existed. Now people are too busy searching for mingei-like items that are not worth even mentioning. It is not an object's shape alone that demands attention, but the extent to which it is deep rooted must also be considered.

June 12, 1927

Dear Leach,

We have decided to have the show by you, Murray, and Mrs. Mairet in the autumn, perhaps in October or November at the Kyū-kyo-dō Gallery. If you could have the goods arrive at the gallery by the beginning of September, it would be convenient for us. We are not concerned about the season so much for the pots, but it is important for the weavings.

I am still in Okinawa with my family and shall not be able to be in Tokyo until the autumn; therefore you had better send the invoice straight to the gallery this time. The director, Mr. K. Kumagai, is quite keen to have the show and is willing to manage the business of customs duty. Yanagi goes to Tokyo once a month now, and Tomi and Tanaka are in the suburbs. We shall meet at the gallery when your works arrive, and are only too pleased to do our best.

The Nihon Mingei Bijutsu-kan (Japan Folkcraft Museum) is going on well. We have collected more than a thousand good things— pots, cloth, metalwork, lacquer, furniture, paintings, prints, and so on. How often we wished you had been there with us when we found a splendid Seto dish, or *kuzu-ori* (rough stuff woven of rags by peasants for their own use), *funadansu* (money chests used in ships), or *Ōtsu-e*. The designs of *soba* cups have great variety and are so fine and interesting. Some of the metalwork and furniture remind me even of Gothic work. I believe the healthy beauty of these crafts in Japan is very much our discovery. It is so different from the so-called beauty of the connoisseurs and modern tea people, yet at the same time we are pleased to find that it shows just the same spirit of the things the first tea-masters chose. We have now come to understand what real craft is and what right craftsmanship is, and Yanagi is even coming to think community work would be the best way to produce real crafts, not work by individual artists (a

91

monastery of craftsmen). He is studying the medieval guilds and their histories with great interest.

We shall have the first exhibition of our collections at the end of this month in Tokyo, and by and by are also going to publish some pamphlets on several subjects, even on foreign crafts, like Yi dynasty furniture or English slipware dishes.

. . . [various business and greetings] . . .

Yours very sincerely,

S. Hamada

Leach:

When Hamada and Yanagi arrived in 1929, they visited Dartington Hall and met Dorothy and Leonard Elmhirst, its founders, with whom I had already begun what became a lifelong friendship. The Elmhirsts had a beautiful marriage—Leonard was a man of culture with vision and ability as an administrator; Dorothy had strong cultural interests and great wealth. Leonard had been the poet Rabindranath Tagore's adviser in agricultural and rural economy at his university at Santiniketan. Dorothy met him there, and they decided to marry and use her wealth to develop a fine English estate to its utmost, culturally as well as agriculturally—that was and is Dartington Hall. I know that Yanagi's words with Leonard had an influence upon him.

Hamada, Yanagi, and I stayed with Henry Bergen in London, and one day Yanagi, across the breakfast table, said, "There are tickets for us to go to Paris by air tomorrow. Come along, let's go and see what Paris is like, let's see what they have been doing, what their painters are doing".

I have forgotten where we stayed in Paris. It was not a very expensive place in the Latin Quarter, but it was comfortable enough and everything was an adventure. Very soon we took a bus out to Chartres. Never shall I forget that day. That sight of the twin spires of Chartres Cathedral miles away over the rolling plain, the land dipping and then rising again, and then finally the ravine and the rise to that great Gothic building of Europe. I am fond of relating this episode, and here will do so again. Yanagi's reaction, spoken to Henry Bergen, Hamada, and myself, is still important. After a long pause, standing before those twin towers and looking at the tall figures, at the bottom of those columns of masonry came the voice of Yanagi saying, "That is what you have lost. That is what you need, a new Gospel." The words sank in, and they have continued to reverberate ever since. I know they had a similar impact on Hamada's mind too. I think now, after all these years, that what Yanagi really meant was that here before us was the physical expression of a common agreement about the meaning of life, of work, and of adoration.

It was Hamada who remarked during his 1929 visit that we should both begin to train assistants. There were no traditional potters in this area—no one who from childhood had learned his craft and had inherited the power of a specific tradition and who would adapt himself under reasonable leadership to very fine expression. Provided the leader does not insist on mere copying on the one hand or self-conscious creative artistry on the other, an innate feeling for truth and beauty may express itself, I believe, in any good modern workshop. We decided to train likely local lads leaving school at fourteen. Our first was Bill Marshall, who is still with us after thirty-six years. In Mashiko there were still traditional craftsmen left, and Hamada has been able to use some assistance, but he chose to train the two throwers who have spent their lives with him.

It has been a constant search to find a true way to combine artist-craftsmen as leaders with a team of usually ex-art-school students. This problem is now world-wide. In former times the inspiration of traditional craftsmen—or leaders of groups of craftsmen—was simply the right way of making an article as it should be made in the service of life; not the expression of beauty for beauty's sake, but beauty for life's sake. Utility and beauty were one and the same.

Hamada in his way in Japan and I in mine here in England have for half a century been trying to find the answer to this problem. I have tried to find his answer in his own words in the tapes made for this book. A solution should be obtainable, but it requires rare humility on both sides—in the leader and in the team. With folk art one is not concerned with who made something. It is the question of the life in the object. When Hamada was asked why he does not sign his own pots, he said, "If you cannot see who it is by, it is either because the pot is bad, or because you are blind." He was then asked why he signs the boxes, and his reply was, "I cannot escape the social obligation." He explained that it should not be a question of whether or not the pot is signed, but of the spirit in which it is made.

Hamada:

My glazing and decorating experience is parallel to that of calligraphy. The best of the calligraphers, I find, are not writing with the brush tip, nor are they conscious of how well the letters are formed. In fact, a good calligrapher is really writing properly when he is writing from the upper arm, nearest to the heart. You can see in his writing when he was relaxed and happy doing it. No matter how the script is formed—sometimes he even makes mistakes—reading it produces a good feeling. I receive many letters of thanks, many from those who have a very fine hand and are conscious of their skill or ways of expression, but I prefer those letters that come straight from the heart, unskilful and clumsy as they may be.

When I was younger I wanted to understand the people who wrote well with a brush, not a pen, like a butterfly wing—why they put writing at the height of artistic expression, as in China. I couldn't understand while I was in Europe. Now I am talking about some of the reasons why I think that it is not the intellect that should be used. Once you have done something with your body, with the whole being, the whole body, then I feel that you are getting somewhere in understanding and that you are in it.

Yanagi talked more and more clearly, towards the end of his life, about using an unmarked foot rule; such marks are intellectual marks, and we must measure things without marks on the ruler. He also said another thing: no compromise;

in this world there is no compromise, in this world one does not measure beauty. Reality and beauty were to him synonymous. He said it is this non-compromise, this spirit of non-compromise, that he felt was the focal point around which all his discussions with his friends rotated. That is why his friends could remain individuals, and they could remain themselves and at the same time they could grow with each other in friendship. Without this level of discussion they could not have grown in their independent ways and still have remained on the same plane at the same time.

Quite often a person who is very facile lacks a deep sense of form. There are a few potters, including two or three who have become famous, who have this special facility. But quite often their form—the body of the pot—is not good; their attention is directed only to the "clothes", the dressing. "Body" and "clothes" should go together. Such potters should pay more attention to the body of the pot—the clay. Critics often like these skilful, clever people very much, but I cannot agree.

It is no use to imitate what has been done in the past; there is no pride, no interest in that. If a potter comes out with new forms, and it is only natural that he should do so, there would be much more feeling of adventure and discovery. You eat your food, and when it has come into your body and been digested, it has no form, it is just a part of you. But it is from first having assimilated nourishment that you come out with some growth, that is, form. But those people who are sharp, clever, or especially gifted with a spontaneous faculty—able to grasp something immediately and directly and without going through this process of digestion and assimilation—are able to react with this imitative flair immediately, and usually the result is not their own. It is merely a mirror reflection and becomes nothing more than an imitation. Of course, this facility may be very helpful at first, but at the same time it does not mean that something is born. Facile imitation does not allow an object to be born, it is only made, and here is the big difference. Usually the outcome is that the maker himself becomes tired and bored with his efforts—not just tired of them, possibly ashamed of them. This quality is often thought of as talent, but talent is different. Many mistakes may be made by not recognizing the difference.

I now think that it is unnecessary to put your seal or stamp on your work before you have reached one tenth of your potting life. This could be interpreted as irresponsible or arrogant. I admit that during my days in Kyoto and my stay in England I did seal my works with a stamp, and even stamped the "S.I." seal of the Leach Pottery on my pots. I have since had other thoughts about this. In Mashiko, to stamp my initials or seal on my pots quite naturally faded from my mind. I have subsequently received sharp reprimands from people because I did not stamp my expensive exhibition pots, and was attacked as being irresponsible. But it must be remembered that according to Japanese custom the Japanese purchasers always buy a box for this type of pot, and I must sign the lid as well as put my stamp on it. The box lid authenticates the pot by Japanese tradition, so it is unnecessary to stamp the pot as well. This leaves me free.

Leach:

The point is that folk art came out of communal life, which is excessively difficult for the individual to grasp and impossible to express. Egotism has to be obliterated, then the pot belongs to everybody, and everybody is a creator. This is why we can feel the impersonal beauty of traditional arts. Then what is the beauty of either a Rembrandt or a Michelangelo—is that impersonal? No, it is highly personal, but beyond egotism.

The inspiration of good craftsmanship in folk art lay not so much with the individual and his special born gifts, but in a community with common standards and the desire for a norm of rightness, whether in making a pot or ploughing a field. The situation we are discussing is comparable with that of the farmer and his labourers. But today even the farmer's labour is done to a large extent by the machine, and the farmer is acquiring a general education. Thus it looks as if the future "good pot" is likely to be made in the main by the special gifted craftsman, whom we must call an artist.

Yanagi wrote much on this most important problem of the place of the artist-potter today. His thinking is complex and derives heavily from his Buddhist studies. In a few words, in Yanagi's "kingdom of beauty", all sit equal at the round table with neither a top nor sides, provided they have rid themselves of egotism and thus received the invitation to the feast. Hamada is concerned about the role of the artist-craftsman today and believes in using the power of healthy traditions as a source and spring-board.

Hamada:

Yanagi's first visit to England was in 1929, and he was simply overwhelmed by the exhibition of English medieval pottery at the Guildhall Museum. He immediately began negotiating with the curator of the museum to swap some articles to exhibit in Japan. This was not possible because the Guildhall was not interested in an exhibition of Japanese material at that time. After the founding of the Japan Folkcraft Museum and many negotiations, thirty-two years later, in 1961, the folkcraft museum opened a loan exhibit of English medieval pottery in Tokyo. These wares resemble the roots of an aged tree in a virgin forest; they urge the potter to preserve them as objects of worship.

Observing things made in previous ages, especially the medieval period, is another way of looking, another way of appreciating. Take, for instance, eating an apple. The primitives took it right off the tree and ate it, skin, seeds, and all. But today we seem to think that peeling it looks better, and then we cut it up and stew it and make a jam of it and prepare it in all kinds of ways. In preparing the apple, quite often we commit many errors on the way. But in just taking it off the tree and eating the whole thing, there are no mistakes to be made. I feel this is a good analogy of the kind of situation we have today.

Yanagi, because the concept of mingei was new, had to make a collection. He had to show all sorts of examples to bring forward a single point, a single conclusion, to allow people to use this conclusion as a standpoint. He had to use a formula for folk art to illustrate the point that he was trying to make. But it was quite clear to Yanagi that this formula was not meant to be followed exactly in our time and age.

When observing works of the past, it is good to have this standard that he set up; it is helpful to have a means with which to observe, to appreciate. But when it comes to producing, to creating for tomorrow, for those who are artists in need of producing, what is written and formulated about folk art is not enough. If this point is not understood, mingei of tomorrow cannot survive. I am saying that Yanagi knew this and yet he did go on with his thesis. The over-attachment to the formulation Yanagi made of folkcraft is what is causing the deterioration, the dying out of mingei these days.

Kawai was not what one would call a purely mingei potter. He was always a man of great freedom. Some time ago I wrote about Kawai and I remember describing him as a crane who had a nest in a tall tree on a high mountain. He came down one day to the lakeside, to join us down below and share our food. He spent some years sharing food with us, then he went off on his own again, flying back by himself. That is how I feel about Kawai's work. People call him mingei, folkcraft, but he is quite different.

Just to give oneself up to folk art will never do. One must chew and eat up mingei—eat it, consume it, put it in your belly; to put it in your system and digest it is what is required in this day and age. We are to assimilate it and do something of our own with this food.

As with Kawai, many have come to folk art and stayed for a while and then have left it. Tomimoto spent rather a brief period there and at one time he put great force and understanding into mingei. Yanagi, towards the latter part of his life, said that in order to tread on the true path of mingei we must have both individual artists and the creative critic to be the pilots, to open the road. When this happens, when the creative critic and the individual artist together open the path, the folk art formula alone is insufficient.

In the past it was unnecessary to assert character or personality—things went on quite well without one's having to do so. But in our age it is quite different. Yanagi quite clearly states this. And to discover one's own true nature and to express it—if realized in the right way—is not different or inconsistent with mingei. According to Yanagi, it is the same road.

This is a strange thing. It might seem as if individual expression and folkcraft are contradictory, but both can be one and the same thing, the same path. If this point is not made clear, Westerners will misunderstand mingei, because generally they think that if the folkcraft formula is not followed, then an object is not mingei. If people do not understand this point, they have not understood the concept of mingei.

Yanagi did not stop merely at folk art, and this point must be made very clear to everyone. When Yanagi criticized the individual artists of today, he was not denying them or negating their right to individual development. People seem not to understand this point either. Of course, Yanagi himself did not explain this position at the beginning; but later on he did say strongly that the powers of the creative critic and the artist must be well combined and that this combination was very much needed in this day and age. Of course this is true, but I emphasize that this need will be even stronger in the future.

Leach asks whether the roots of all the mingei things handed down to us today and of today's individual artists' works are not joined, are not one. Yes, I would agree that this is so, but it is not what is seen on the surface that counts, but what is not seen. This root is what matters. In the root, the unseen root, the real power, the real strength of an object lies. One must never judge by what can be seen on the surface only.

In choosing craftsmen to be designated "Living National Treasures" in Japan, the first criterion was whether the person had been able to preserve the past essence of a particular craft. But an enlightened man in the Education Ministry responsible for giving out the money suggested that this criterion alone would not do, but that the person must show some sign of individuality, some sign of new design—new ideas must be present in his work in order to be worthy of this prize.

The root may be firmly planted in tradition, but when it buds, when it branches out on the surface, it must be fresh and new. This wise man in the Education Ministry felt that such people must be chosen to become Living National Treasures, otherwise the designation would not have any value for the future.

Magosaburō Ōhara, the man whose European art and folkcraft collections are now housed in Kurashiki and who helped finance Yanagi's folkcraft museum, was once given a huge dish of mine. He had it in his study and began to complain that he could not do any work because of that dish—his eyes were always being drawn to it, and it was bothering him, he said, because he was being diverted—it was so powerful. "I refuse to be defeated by this plate," he said, so he got another one and he put it next to the first. And he placed a third one there. Then, he stated, he was enlightened.

It was not the number of plates; he got as many as he could. "Please keep sending me more, as many as you can," he requested, and altogether he ended up with more than twenty or twenty-five. But his challenge, his way of accepting the pots, impressed me very much. He tackled the objects like he tackled people. He was wrestling with pots, and his attitude towards them was very refreshing.

It is rare to come across such a man. He was not looking at the pots as a collector; I feel that Ōhara did not have a real eye for pots, but more important, Ōhara was looking at the man behind the objects. He was not just a collector or lover of pots; he was trying to see me, the maker of the things. This really shows the worth of the man; few people talk about or see objects like this. Ōhara was using pots to understand the person who made them and thus to understand himself.

Whatever one sees is a reflection of oneself. Without you there is not the objective world or the subjective—the object never exists without the subject. This is not taught in schools; this is what the cuckoo taught me on the cliffs in Cornwall.

Introduction by Sōetsu Yanagi to catalogue of Hamada exhibition, Paterson Gallery, November, 1931

In the long history of pottery in Japan, many distinguished potters have come and gone, with all their varied styles and skill. Shōji Hamada is a new and advancing figure among living potters, and a few words in description of his unique position in the world of ceramics today may not be out of place as an introduction to this catalogue.

Up to the present, almost all modern potters have wasted their talents on technique. Rare glazes, new colour effects, and novelties of form have been their chief aims; their highest ambition has been to do something that other artists have never done and could never have done. It has seemed to them that there is no better way of astonishing the world. But why should one want to astonish the world?

Hamada, on the contrary, recognized almost from the very beginning, and the conviction has grown upon him throughout his career, that beauty can never be attained by sophistications of technique, for beauty is a thing of soundness and truth. Rejecting the insincerities and over-refinements of mere technical dexterity, he has gone back to the three sources from which the health that is inherent in all beauty springs; and although these sources may seem very homely and plain (and indeed it is because of their very simplicity that most modern artist-potters do not understand them), nevertheless the way that Hamada has chosen will one day be regarded as the beginning of a renaissance in the art of the individual potter.

First he has recognized that the beauty of pottery is almost wholly dependent on good natural materials. This should indeed be the fundamental conviction of every potter. Most potters, however, abuse their materials in the endeavour towards mechanical elaboration and refinement and turn out finished products regardless of any organic connection between the objects and the substances of which they are made. Few understand that the beauty of ceramics is mainly the beauty of materials. They prefer to trust rather to their own technical knowledge and dexterity than to the natural qualities of clay. But how much better it would be for them to be able to make use of the raw gifts of nature than to be carried away by the delusion that nature can be refined and improved upon by sophistication. Actually no handcraft has ever arisen where no good natural materials exist. The reason why until now Hamada has worked sometimes in Okinawa in the south and at other times in the potters' village of Mashiko in the north is because he has found that the natural clays and glazes of both these districts are well suited to his work. To him the making of pottery is not a matter of secret chemical formulas but simply one of openly putting to use the common materials of the earth.

In the second place, he has recognized that the beauty of pottery finds its fullest expression only when it is joined to utility. This signifies a return from the idea of pottery as an article of luxury to one of practical use, its removal, in other words, from the parlour to the living room and the kitchen. Modern artist-potters forget that the aim of handcrafts is primarily concerned with utility, not ornament; and they apparently believe that nothing can possess nobility or dignity if made for common use. The very idea is an insult to their aesthetic sensibilities. They forget that all the best of the old pieces, which we value so highly today, were made not for ornament but for the ordinary purposes of the household, and the healthiness of their beauty tells us what faithful friends they once were in the domestic life of men long since departed. To make sound stoneware that can be of actual service in the home is what Hamada is aiming at. He is one of the few moderns who love the beauty of the traditional arts of the people.

These two considerations have naturally led him to the third, which I believe he will be able to carry out more completely in the future. It is the endeavour to restore the making of pottery to its former position as an open craft in which anyone may share. Many artists boast of their ability to make things that others cannot make; beauty, however, can and should be found rather in the simplest and commonest of objects. If an artist can discover why the simple products of some old traditional craft become beautiful independently of any idiosyncrasy of decoration or of the individuality of any one person, he can make no greater contribution to the attainment of beauty in our daily lives.

It is Hamada's endeavour to draw as close as he can to the world that is natural, common, and simple. Some may regard his pottery as crude and coarse; yet it has been made only after the most careful consideration and thought. Nearly all potters of today are walking precariously like acrobats on a tight-rope in their desire to do something extraordinary, whereas Hamada only wishes to make plain the truth that the most healthy and natural beauty comes from simplicity. No modern potter seems ever to have thought, much less to have done what he is doing. For to build up solidly on these simple foundations is an almost impossible undertaking for the sophisticated individualistic potter of today, who is desirous of distinguishing himself by doing something unusual. Those who are without wisdom and will cannot hope to stand firm against the many temptations that surround them; for in the long run the problem of beauty is the problem of conscience.

The work of Shōji Hamada stands solidly upon mother earth. That one can see in the sturdy, cheerful forms of his pots. He has just completed building his kiln in Mashiko; and everyone who knows him believes in his work, for his way lies on the open road away from danger.

S. Yanagi

Leach:

In 1934 I was invited to return to Japan, and Yanagi begged me to bring a batch of slipware, which I had not made for some years. Later on he wrote a criticism, saying, "Leach's stoneware we admire, but we love his slipware, born not made." This went home rather deep, and is not unrelated to what I have said about modern pots in general. So I made another attempt to produce some of this middle-temperature slipware, which is so English.

At St. Ives we had ceased to produce slipware because we felt we could not do too many things using different glazes, different clays, different kiln firings, and so forth. It was an unsatisfactory and unprofitable use of our energies as potters, and, after all, stoneware is less porous and more durable than slipware. Yanagi's statement about my previous slipware, that gentle but penetrating "born not made", lingered in my mind. One other reason why I chose to concentrate on stoneware was that my inspiration was from an Orient hitherto unknown, just as Yanagi's request for English slipware was a borrowing from, to him, an alien culture.

I went to Mashiko and saw what Hamada had been making during the interval of eleven years. His work struck me as stark and with very little influence from English wares. Later, when I saw him and we talked and talked, he agreed that he had thrown away as much as possible to assure integration with only that which had become a part of him. This was his process of digestion. In consequence, amongst all his pots I recollect none that could be described as an imitation. This was a display of Hamada's sagacity, even in his earlier years. I have seen many Mashiko pots, of the kind that were produced for the kitchens of Tokyo, and they had always seemed rather plain, honest, not full of artistry or striving after beauty. To me, at that time, it appeared odd that a man with such unusual capacity and sensibility as Hamada seemed not to be utilizing fully the artistic talents with which he is so highly gifted. Now, after many years, I see his wisdom. What is *empty* can be filled. The simplicity of the Mashiko ware left Hamada free to make his own statements, statements that have the person-less quality—and beauty—we find in nature throughout all its manifestations. This, I think, is a noble kind of art, yet it is nothing more or less than normal.

Hamada:

Mashiko clay is not the best in quality, and I was advised by many people when I first went there to order better clay. But I was satisfied with the Mashiko clay just as I was content with the purity of Mashiko. Thanks to this difficult clay, it took me only twenty years to completely acclimatize myself to the conditions in Mashiko. If I had been confronted with a better quality clay, it might have taken me longer. I prefer making quality work from inferior clay to producing inferior pieces from quality clay.

Let me elaborate on clay. Formerly, kilns were erected near clay deposits. This was especially so during feudal times in Japan when strict control was exercised to avoid even the slightest leak of secret materials or formulas from one fief to another. The potters were very competitive.

In this age, however, all types of clay are available from suppliers. It is my belief that when you discover a natural clay that suits your work, you should immediately pack up and move to the place where that clay is available. Clay is that important. Glaze and decorative painting easily capture people's eyes and cause them to overlook the most important material—clay. Considering the nature of pottery, the primary consideration is the selection of the clay.

The thing to remember is that the simplest clay is the best. Don't mix it and try to make it complex; one kind of clay is all you need. Clay itself is already the most complex of mixtures because it is alive, a living thing. Man's intellect cannot produce a natural material—man's ability to perceive is not fine or sensitive enough to take in what nature has to give.

The first thing to remember is to keep the clay in its simplest form. It must have the right kind of stickiness and plasticity—body and bone—and must be strong in the fire. These qualities must be inherent in the clay. Many potters are concerned about the colour of the clay and search for light or buff-coloured clays, but I think the colour is of secondary importance. I can tell the plasticity of a clay by handling it, but to find out what I can do with that particular clay and know its limitations requires throwing and experimenting with it.

If it is possible even in this modern day and age to be able to find a place with the right clay deposit, then the potter should have his pottery and kiln there.

Today potting is like a department store; clay is bought by sending a postcard to any area of the world and asking for a particular clay and getting it in a few days. The department store kind of society is likely to insist that a potter use whatever kind of clay is popular or in demand, whatever colour is popular. Don't be whipped around by such a demand; resist that kind of pressure. This is most important. If you find the clay, make the kiln right where the clay is and do the work. This is a fundamental thing. These days it is very difficult to do such simple things because conditions are so complicated.

Now you have some clay before you, what can you do with this ordinary, normal throwing clay? Try to make a dish, a cup; try to make bowls. Then go on to larger pieces. In the beginning you start with something round, because you are throwing on the wheel. Then you can press in two sides and get an eliptical shape. This is the most simple, fundamental technique. It is not just an attempt at irregularity. A bowl will carry liquids better if it has pressed sides because the contents will not spill easily—this is for *use*. Then you can go on to pressing or patting four sides, then six. Three sides are very difficult; three or five sides are rather rare, though they are found in Japan. With eight sides, there is no place for the clay to contract, and you can hardly see the flat sides that are being pressed. In such cases, usually I throw a thicker wall and then cut the eight or more sides.

You can make many shapes and variations out of the one clay with different techniques—with coiling, throwing, and with slabs, in which you cut pieces and lute them together. Also you can carve a box and lid out of a block of clay. Tomimoto made many porcelain boxes in this way. Even with a single clay you can think of perhaps twenty ways of making shapes.

If you have a red or a dark clay, when it is fired it gets even darker in colour; what can you do about that? Use a white slip to cover the surface. Quite often you can find such white clay in the same area as a dark clay deposit. Some potters are afraid of a white slip coating because it may peel off the body, but if you leave a roughish surface on the pot, the slip grips that surface and usually does not flake off. You also might like hakeme. With a contrasting slip, you can add ten more ways of making shapes and patterns. This sort of thing is not taught much in schools; people do not talk about simple and obvious methods. There are also some things you can do when the clay is wet, rather on the soft side, as well as some methods you can use when the clay is half-dry.

One can think of many ways of decorating a pot with one or two contrasting slips. The English medieval slipware dishes are an outstanding example of slip trailing. The Mashiko tea-pot is a good example of dipping a round pot into a pan of slip, producing a round circle on the side of the pot. A pattern can be put in this circle.

Another technique is inlay. The pot, when it is medium hard, can be decorated by scratching lines, pressing a stamp or roller into the clay, or a short length of wet cord or rope can be rolled on the pot, leaving an impressed pattern. The pot is then brushed with or dipped in a contrasting slip. After the slip has dried a bit, the surface of the pot is scraped with a flat blade, leaving the contrasting colour in the indentations.

One method we use often in our workshop is to beat the clay with textured wooden paddles. This technique was first used by primitive potters when they made very large coiled pots. The beating strengthened the joints between coils. When beating the clay with a paddle, at first the water is absorbed into the wood and wears away the softer parts, etching the grain deeper with time and use. Also paddling can be used to make small flat surfaces on a rounded pot. There were two types of old paddles used: one with the wood grain straight, the other was from wood sawn obliquely, giving a concentric grain pattern. Old paddles are better than new ones. The paddle grips and tightens the clay as you beat it. Although the texture thus impressed in the clay can be smoothed over, I prefer to leave the impressed pattern on the pot to produce a textured surface that holds the glaze well in its depressions.

In the Jōmon period, they used such paddles, and the archaeologists like to separate what they call the circular pattern and the straight-grained pattern. This is just nonsense; each pattern simply comes from whichever old paddle has been used. It was not contrived at all, it was just their way of making pots.

An interesting example of how a technique or process creates its own pattern is the chatter-mark pattern made by a "jumping iron". This is a springy, curved strip of very light iron (the early Chinese tool was bent bamboo) with an end squared like a chisel. This strip is held loosely in the fingers, and the chisel end of the iron is brought down at right angles to the surface of the slowly turning slip-covered pot. "Jumping" over the clay surface, the iron creates parallel chatter marks, removing a touch of slip at each jump and so exposing the clay underneath. The interesting thing is that the bowl or pot is naturally a bit drier on the upper part and rim, so that the tool makes a narrow nick at the top, which widens to a firmer, more decisive stroke on the lower part. The process has done this, not the potter.

Combining and exploring all the very simple techniques indicated here alone will produce about fifty varieties of pots. No one has ever explored all of the infinite variations of these simple techniques.

Also a stencil pattern made from paper, leather, cloth, etc. can be wetted and stuck onto the pot before it is dipped or brushed with slip. It will peel off as the pot dries, leaving a sharp, clearly defined pattern outline.

The technique of sgraffito alone is an endless source of patterns, especially if it is combined with a glaze-over-glaze technique. Some Okinawan traditional ware is a good example of this technique.

Most potters think that unless they put specific patterns or drawings on the pot they are not making a pattern. They should realize that the pattern was being created from the very beginning of the pot-making process; the material itself creates the pattern. The potter must learn to see and to recognize this.

The most important point is that the use of the clay and slip themselves bring out a pattern—this is the correct way of creating pattern. I think that this is a terribly important point, especially for the Western potter, who tends to think of material and decoration as two separate things.

Around the third year of my work at the Kyoto Testing Institute I began to realize that there are two kinds of patterns to consider: the natural ones that come from the material itself and the kind that is intellectually conceived.

Leach:

Working at Mashiko in 1934, I had a room that was one wing of the gateway to Hamada's land. Such gateways, or gate-houses, are noticeable in the architecture of that part of Japan, Tochigi Prefecture. The gate itself is flanked by rooms on either side, which are traditionally used as living quarters or for storage; the roof is beautifully thatched. The room on the left on entering had been apportioned to me, with a wheel set up for me to work on, and an assistant from the village of potters, trained in throwing, a young and vigorous man ready to do what I asked him.

I have called Hamada's work plain. During the 150 years of the existence of this potters' village called Mashiko, the glazes had been developed out of local raw materials, as is true of every pottery village in Japan. Mashiko ware was just plain, ordinary, decent kitchen ware. This simplicity and bareness I also found in Hamada's work. The simple range of natural materials available to him in Mashiko was a self-imposed limitation, considering his profound knowledge of glazes and ceramic chemistry. It is one of the most extraordinary and remarkable things, to my mind, that he has been able to take the ordinary local material without effort and use it so freely that the result becomes extraordinary.

Hamada:

In my early days at Mashiko a good friend and adviser wanted me to make a test. What he wanted me to do was to take Kawai's Kyoto materials and use them in Mashiko, and take Mashiko materials to Kyoto and use them there, and then show him the results. The question in his mind was how much the kiln influenced the pots. Did the character of the kiln play the major role, and would Mashiko's rough clay become "Kyoto-ised"?

The results were not good. I did not like them. We learned that the kiln had

103

a great deal of effect. The next point my friend advised was, "Now you, Hamada, go to Kyoto and make something, and take Kawai to Mashiko and have him do work there. Then compare." The result was that when I worked in Kyoto, the work produced there was very much "à la Kyoto"—the difference was both in materials and kiln. Everyone was surprised at what came out of my work and that I could produce something Kyoto-like. But if you really looked deeply, there was not so much difference; the work was still Hamada, but hidden underneath. Ultimately there was no real difference. The difference was only on the surface.

Hamada working in Mashiko was the best—Hamada going to Kyoto, not bad. The worst thing was to transfer materials from Kyoto to Mashiko; nothing was gained using Kyoto materials in Mashiko. Kawai came to Mashiko and worked with the Mashiko materials—the result was very good. Moving the materials to a different locality and working there produced the most unnatural results. We learned that if you find a particular material is good in a certain locality you must take yourself to that place; do not uproot the material and use it elsewhere. Even if such a move is impossible for you, it is important to recognize the truth of this law.

Previously my busy schedule in Mashiko did not permit me to visit Okinawa as much as I wanted. I remember the delightful experience of living in Okinawa with my wife and son for more than a year. The sugar-cane fields stretching endlessly in front of my workshop inspired me to create a pattern, which has continued to capture my interest, to my surprise, for these many years, without my becoming tired of it.

I drew the cane leaves, stem, and top as they appear after being stricken by the violence of a typhoon. My style of drawing this pattern has changed naturally with the years, and my good friends tell me that they can detect changes in this sugar-cane pattern about every ten years. Now this pattern has become my trademark. Many people have copied this and others. Since I have many patterns and designs, I have never paid attention to the copies. Leach said I should protest, and I jokingly told him that it is my belief that if people imitated my designs for a hundred years, among the copies there should be at least a few good designs showing the good side of me, which would supplement my defects.

To completely master the techniques of the potter's wheel one must have a good wheel and practise repeatedly. That is the best and the only way. After much practice, rice bowls or teabowls of the same size with the same amount of clay should begin to look larger. When you throw a bowl on the wheel, it is my conviction that the top rim should never appear cut off or finished where work has stopped. If it continues to rise in feeling, the inside of a bowl will begin to look much larger than its outside. The centre of gravity is heightened, and the bowl appears much lighter than its actual weight. It should never look heavier to the eye than it feels when it is picked up. That is very unpleasant.

The turning of the base and footring of a bowl is regarded the most difficult.

Excess clay must be removed to lighten the bowl and facilitate firing, and the turned footring stabilizes the entire piece. Turning must be as natural as one's approach to materials and other techniques. It must be remembered that the pot is very soft when it is being thrown and turned and, again, when it is firing in the kiln it gets soft once more. Sometimes, depending on the clay, the pot gets almost as soft as molten glass. Any good potter knows that a footring must be thick enough to hold the weight of the whole pot during firing. When the pot has a lid as well, the footring must be strong enough to support that weight too. The form, the weight, the action of the fire must all be considered in making the footring, and as you become more experienced you know exactly how much clay to turn off the foot. You know instinctively, physically, what to do.

More and more as time went by, potters tried to be fanciful and tried to make different footrings. The Japanese, especially the people of Tea, were doing this. But the development of the potter is measured by how naturally he can make a footring, how he knows what goes into a footring and the use of it. He uses his total experience, he is one with the bowl itself, and the question of how naturally and how alive that footring is depends on how much he is a part of the article he is making.

However, in the long course of history, the methods of removing the excess clay and turning the footring are not identical in each nation: the Koreans remove the clay quickly and abruptly; the Chinese powerfully. As a young potter I was rather reckless and ignorant; I tried all the tricks on the foot. When I became a little older, I felt the urge to show my proficiency by making the foot rather roughly, then I tried to be sentimental and treated the foot gently. I tried all methods; each was easily detected by those doing the same thing.

But strangely enough, when I was about fifty, I started to realize that the most natural way of making the foot was better than any fancy methods. You are your own person if you can turn the foot in a natural manner unselfconsciously. I think the footring relates to the "year rings" of a potter's growth.

As might be expected, the early great masters of the Tea ceremony discovered the key to the exquisiteness of the footring. But the pottery artists, on the other hand, were carried away in the pursuit of mere artificiality by shaping fancy, novel, and unusual footrings. However, the more able potters managed in their later years to produce the most natural and treasured footrings unself-consciously. Usually they were in their sixties before they accomplished this.

The Chinese and Koreans are interesting. The Chinese are skilful and good; they can turn a footring quickly and make it truly live. The Koreans don't mind anything; they are casual and are not concerned at all about how they do things. They know what the pot needs and they do it.

Whether the pot is crooked or not is not important to the Koreans; they turn off large chunks of clay—sometimes the foot is uneven, and often the bowl is even better because of it. It is the Japanese who evaluate these things and are aware of the high quality of beauty involved in the freshness of the Korean pots. Then they try to imitate this natural unevenness, and this is where they fall short, defeated.

There is a story that compares the three countries, China, Japan, and Korea. A boy is standing on the beach and throwing stones over the water. The boy represents the Chinese; he can throw stones the furthest because he has the force and skill. Then comes the Japanese, who sees the boy throwing a stone and wants to imitate him. He throws a stone, but it falls short of the Chinese. The Korean is like a woman or little girl who sees the two others throwing and wants to join in the game. She throws with all her might, and the stone falls short, but she does not mind; she enjoys the game.

The three countries are somewhat like that. In the early stages the Chinese could throw farther because they had a natural force—they were able to do this without any special effort. The Japanese, on the other hand, do not have that natural force, so the stone may not, in the beginning, reach so far. But in spite of this, because they are skilful and persevere, they ultimately come to the point where they can throw as far as the Chinese. The Japanese must do a lot of hard work and practise to get to that point. The Koreans enjoy themselves whether they make it or not; they have no idea of achieving or not achieving. The Japanese soon learn that if they choose a particular kind and shape of stone carefully, they can throw it as far as the Chinese. Then they can learn to imitate the little girls of Korea and say, "Now this is what the Koreans do." But here is where the Japanese go wrong. They know, and they can distinguish the two styles, and they make a self-conscious effort to do so. But they are the worst of the three, or rather the least good, because they are able to do the Chinese style and do the Korean style—in fact they are very proud of this skill, but this becomes their only Japanese style. This is not just true in the potting world, it is true in every direction of Japanese development.

When the Koreans make pots, they take the pot off the wheel at a different time than we do. They throw from a lump of very soft clay. The clay is so soft and the throwing so fast that the bowl is actually held up by the centrifugal force of the wheel. They must cut it off very quickly, otherwise it would deform and collapse.

The clay is still extremely soft when they turn the footring. They are making very cheap ware and they work so quickly that often the pot is not perfectly centred or level for turning. Sometimes this results in one side of the footring being thinner than the other. This is the "quarter moon" footring that the Japanese appreciate so much, but of course when the Japanese potters try to do it on purpose. . . ! If you look at the early Karatsu ordinary ware, plain rice bowls, etc., you can see that they are off-centre a bit.

I have tried myself to turn footrings when the clay is very soft, like the Koreans. I found that my metal turning tools stuck to the soft clay and I had to use a wooden or bamboo tool as they did.

When the clay is so soft, the pebbles in rough clay stand out or are pulled out. Sometimes the turned area is so rough that it must be smoothed a bit before glazing, but the Japanese like the ones that were not smoothed and did not take the glaze perfectly. We call this crepe-like surface "frogs' eggs". It is the Ido effect.

The Korean Ido teabowls, highly treasured as the masterpieces of master-pieces for generations by the Tea masters, were originally made as ordinary bowls to hold food and wine. They were so cheaply made and widely sold that no one knows where they first originated. For instance, if two hundred Ido tea-bowls were made in a day, it means that more than six thousand pieces were made in a month. Such a potter would produce countless numbers of these pots in his lifetime. The key to solve the mysteries of Ido teabowls is to know how many pieces a potter can make in his lifetime. This I do not know and . . . I fail to make anything as good.

But it is interesting to note that the foot, which is so important, is hidden be-neath the pot. A man may appraise the foot by just picking up the teabowl and holding it upside down. Many people know where to look, but only a few know what to appreciate. Knowing and appreciating are not the same. Knowing things sometimes impedes the power of true observation. Those who can see with their own eyes are truly fortunate. Such seeing can lead to other discoveries and other creations.

Leach:

From Mashiko we went over to the Funaki family's Fujina Pottery on the shore of Lake Shinji, on the other side of Japan and considerably further south. The old city of Matsue stands on the two sides of the lake's exit to the sea, with a feudal castle on one side and one bridge across the narrow opening to the sea. The Funakis have been making pottery for some centuries. The whole of that area had been the fief of the Matsudaira family, a very famous one in feudal Japan.

At this pottery a tradition exists of using lead added to the usual higher tem-perature glazes. By adding a small percentage of lead, the firing temperature of the traditional glazes could be reduced to around 1,100° C. Thus it became possi-ble to closely imitate the lead-glazed rural red wares of England. So it was that Hamada after his return had showed them how to do this, and when I visited them in 1934 I showed them a good deal more of the tradition. The resulting glaze was glassy and transparent and suitable for showing the slip decoration beneath it, trailed, combed, or dipped. The pieces were amberish in colour, friendly, reminiscent of the kitchens and countryside of England. There was loving kindness in them. There was also a strong English influence in shapes.

At Mashiko, Hamada spread by example what he had learned when he was in St. Ives. At the Funaki's Fujina Pottery, he taught the specific techniques that had come from that period of studying in England and working with Eng-lishmen, which he thought would help or which they liked or he encouraged them to like. The Funakis took the opportunity of my visit to learn as much as possible from me (I think Hamada wished me to serve that purpose), and I think my best contribution was in showing them how to make handles.

The pulled handle was unknown in Japan, though the technique was known a little in Korea. This technique involves holding a sort of tapering wedge of clay, a little bit harder than that suitable for throwing on the wheel, milking it with a wet hand as one would a cow's teat, and pulling it out to the right thickness and curvature. Accurately placed, it is both useful and engaging to the user—one wants to feel the nice touch of a good handle when pouring. The Funakis learned the method very quickly, as did the Japanese potters in the half-dozen or so other places where I taught the technique, then and on subsequent visits. I enjoy making a handle, and probably do it better than throwing. Something of the past seems to run through my sensibilities when I feel that tongue of clay slipping through my wet fingers and run its head home into its proper balancing and strengthening position on a pot.

These things, simple though they may sound in words and to teach, are slow to become natural to a potter who has always used cups without handles. It is not a matter of ability, but of experience. For example, the potter in Japan who loves saké naturally makes good saké bottles and cups.

Hamada:

When I returned from England in the spring of 1924 and went to Kawai's, I have never felt more strongly than at that time that I had someone who was waiting for me. I was immensely moved by the trust with which Kawai received everything and how he did his best. Even the dullest bell responded resonantly if Kawai struck it. Whenever I made a trip with Kawai, I experienced double the pleasure—seeing things myself and watching Kawai's enthusiasm. Kawai must have received something from me also, and I am greatly indebted to him for his intense ability to receive, which has helped me to clarify the way that I have followed.

With Yanagi, things in his room become quiet under his influence. His choice and associations are, in a sense, his creation, and through him articles come to have their own character. In contrast, Kawai was influenced by things; he was an appreciator of things, yet they continue their own independent existence. Books, Kawai's works, as well as collected objects were carefully arranged and kept spotless. Love towards and from articles helped create a unique atmosphere of busyness, which prevailed throughout his place, and you could not tell his studio from his drawing room or display room. It was the same when he was a youth living in a boarding house. There he neatly displayed his books and works, though without shelves; the room served as his studio as well.

Apparently Kawai was fully satisfied and pleased with things he received, rather than taking things from others and putting them to practical use. Probably not a few people who visited Kawai's learned how to love things.

I have known few artists who incorporate what impresses them into their own works more promptly and with greater enthusiasm and aptitude than Kawai did. For instance, he asked someone to copy a Korean inkstone for him, but he could not wait until it was completed, and started making it himself, using the clay he was familiar with. In two or three months, using different techniques, he came out with more than one hundred inkstones, including a few dozen different types.

Constant changes in technique and form to create new works involve technical difficulties, but Kawai seemed to enjoy such challenge in the same way as enjoying sports. He met each challenge with renewed enthusiasm.

A change of clothing is not always followed by internal change. Constant effort to improve the outside does not always help improve the content. An artist who starts his career at the age of forty or fifty has no alternative but to do what he wants in the way suited for him.

Any person who is good at receiving things like Kawai should actively digest and turn those things he has received into his own work. I wish Kawai had explored a way for individual artists that may be called the modern *tariki-dō*—the Way of Receiving a Power from Without. It is pitiful to see many artists today wearing out their nerves by becoming too sensitive to minute differences. There is too much fearful chasing of the unusual or quaint in people's striving to say something "individual". I strongly hope for the great broad way of crafts where an artist achieves his work instinctively and receives—then returns what he likes.

Sometimes Kawai was too enthusiastic in attempting new work. Even when his work looked good to other people, he often was dissatisfied. He was not satisfied unless he went to a point that seemed too far. He once admitted, "It seems that I have something like the mask of a devil that threatens others." It may have been a shortcoming arising from excessiveness.

At one point Kawai started to make more mould-cast pieces. Of course, at first he was inspired by his interest in mould casting. This activity proved to be helpful and advantageous to him because the original mould is modified and freed from the danger of excessiveness through the moulding process, which can be entrusted to others. I believe that if the great broad way of *tariki* for individual artists had evolved, Kawai would have been able to create finer work.

Yet Kawai had much for which I have taken off my hat for many years. Though I admire him, I feel he lost something—or he did not receive fully—and I believe he might have grown more and then would have been appreciated accordingly.

Yanagi never wanted to reject a person when he saw anything good in him. We all felt that Kawai had not done his best work yet, that things were still to come out of him. He had a wonderful way of understanding religion. Yanagi felt that Japan should have a potter who depended upon *tariki*, the Other Power, and felt very much that Kawai might accomplish this.

Quite often when Yanagi visited Kawai, there would be some pots that Kawai himself had rejected out of his own kiln, sometimes a whole yard full of them out in the wind and rain. Then Yanagi would go to those pieces and pick one out and say, "You must not mistreat such a good piece." It was out of batches of rejects that he would take pieces back to the folkcraft museum for display. Kawai was such that criticism dejected him, he could not take it. Yanagi himself felt that such quiet approbation was the most he could do for Kawai.

The kind of mistake people have made about Kawai is that they thought they were shaking his hand but quite often they may have been shaking his foot. Many people think *he* was great, but there are very few who really sincerely say they like Kawai's work.

Iseki said the reason why he understood Kawai so well, in spite of the fact that he could not stand Kawai's work, is that he, too, had a similar weakness and could sympathize. Whenever Iseki saw a newspaper with some bad criticism of Kawai, he always wrote a consoling postcard because he felt the man needed such support.

Iseki said to me, some fifty years ago when I was doing a kiln, "Oh there are Tomimoto's pots, yes, and there are Kawai's, and so forth, but you . . . yours are the best in Japan, no mistake about it. Don't worry." He always encouraged people by telling them the affirmative. This is a very difficult thing to do. You can always criticize people and help them grow, but in the case of Iseki, he said the best thing possible that he could say about that person and encouraged him to grow. He made absolute statements. When he affirmed something he made an absolute affirmation of it. Iseki would say, "I smell something good about Kawai's exhibition this year, maybe I will buy something." He went and bought something and came back and said, "No, this will never do", and then would give the pot away to somebody.

In one of my early exhibitions Iseki came and talked to a man who had come to buy something. "There's a lively pot out there, I think you should buy it." It was one hundred yen in those days, quite a lot of money. He said, "I guarantee it's a good pot, you should get it. I will ask Hamada and have it reduced to seventy-five yen. But if you take it home and are not satisfied with it, I will buy it from you for one hundred yen."

I never heard this story directly from Iseki, but from the manager of the gallery. That's the way Iseki encouraged me. When no one was watching, he silently went about his way to help. It is a rare thing to be flattered or complimented by someone and still be able to grow. These two things do not often go hand in hand. Usually it is easier to be criticized and then try to outgrow that criticism. But to be given warm and hospitable surroundings and yet to be able to grow, this is rare. It is perhaps the best way to grow.

Kawai often would compliment a student on a point that he himself was not able to develop, and it was through the student's particular gift that Kawai ate that knowledge. What he was doing was killing the student by compliments, and quite often the disciple never grew; he just died, withered away, from having been complimented by Kawai. When Kawai complimented, he never helped the other person to grow.

Kawai's work is growing more popular today. I wonder which direction this will lead. Of course there are many, many things in Japan that are less good than Kawai's work. I can well understand that his work is becoming valued, but I just wonder what the result of this will be.

Yanagi, Kawai, and I toured the whole of Korea, north and south, on three occasions during the thirties. Even today markets are still held regularly every week in Korean towns, where the visitor can purchase not only presents and souvenirs but also fine quality goods and wares for everyday use. In the spring of 1937, with the purpose of purchasing such wares in mind, I went to a town in the south of Korea, accompanied by Yanagi and Kawai. In a tea shop I found a bowl used for drinking *makkŏli*, the rough home-made Korean saké, which was identical to a Japanese Tea ceremony bowl. I asked the proprietor to sell the bowl to me. Instead, he brought me a bowl full of *makkŏli*. I told him that it was not the liquor I wanted but the bowl itself. The proprietor's reply was negative. He said the bowl was for his shop and he couldn't sell it. However, he advised me to go to the neighbouring village, where a market was scheduled for the following day and where I could find many similar bowls. I told the proprietor that I could not stay much longer, and finally he acquiesced to my request and told me to come again at five o'clock in the evening. After the tea shop was closed for the day, the proprietor sold me the bowl for five sen. A cup of *makkŏli* was also five sen, so you can see how cheap the bowl was. I then asked the proprietor where the bowl I had just purchased was made. He said that it was at a kiln located not far away. We decided to visit it. We saw a boy about fourteen or fifteen years old with a carrying frame strapped to his back loaded with wood, and asked him where the kiln was located. "You'll come to a small stream in a little while. Go along the stream and cross it three times. Then you'll find it," he replied. What a curious way to give directions. Shards in the stream began to increase in number, and among them we sometimes found excellent broken footrings. We are nearing the kiln, we thought, and went up a hill, from where we obtained a fine view of the surrounding countryside.

We saw rows of straw-thatched houses at the foot of the hill, with a stream winding its way through them. There was an earthen bridge over the stream, on whose banks we could see rows of willows. It was a typical Korean village. What a fine place we have come to, we exclaimed, but we could not find the kiln. In Korea, we had heard that farmers settle the best land, while potters and their families congregate on the top of the hills, where the soil is poor.

But we sensed that we were near the kiln and were happy that we would at last be able to see how Koreans turn the feet of their pots. Yes, there was the kiln, smoke pouring out of it. It was a climbing kiln with seven or eight chambers, and only the upper half was being fired. This was quite contrary to the ordinary concept of firing. I asked them why they were doing such a wasteful thing. They replied that the lower half had been confiscated by the money lender to whom they were in debt. We were astonished and could not imagine that they could fire a kiln this way or make any profit.

Entering the first house, we saw an old man with a flowing beard and wearing a typical Korean hat. He was throwing—slowly. The free way he used the wheel made us wonder if the pieces would be symmetrical. Here is the reason, we thought, that Korean pottery is irregular. Looking at one finished piece he had cut off the wheel, we noticed that there was a hole in the bottom. I asked the old man whether he had made a mistake. He replied no. All the pottery drying outside had such holes. The wife of the old man went outside, turned a piece upside down, and began to paddle it with a flat tool. As she paddled the piece, the clay spread in toward the centre of the bottom and finally filled in and covered the hole. The bottom of a piece was compressed in this way and, without a footring, would be very strong in the fire. Although we had desired very much to see Korean turning, it was not to be at this pottery, to our regret. What we saw did not fully satisfy our desire, but we felt happy that we had at least studied the Korean footring indirectly. (Leach: The footring is often thrown on the bottom of such paddled pieces. This technique avoids the danger of turned footrings cracking because of the difference in moisture between the inside and outside of the foot, and some clay has a very high shrinkage rate.)

We asked the men at the kiln to show us what kinds of things they made and said we wanted to buy some. They were delighted and hauled out many different kinds of pottery, among which were bowls, high-footed vessels, and various small pieces. All were just food vessels in white or black. We wanted to buy all the pottery in view. It was astonishingly cheap. It was so cheap, in fact, that we decided to purchase the whole kiln load. The number of pieces in one firing was about twelve or thirteen hundred, the whole lot of which cost ¥126. We tried to hand them the ¥126, but they said that it was not a good idea for them to have as much as ¥100 in their possession there. They told us to deposit ¥100 at the village office and to give them ¥26. This we did. We left the kiln very satisfied, thinking what a good bargain we had made. But when the shipment arrived, almost every piece was broken. No doubt they did not know how to pack the pottery since it was the first time they had done so. Our purchase, therefore, turned out to be quite an expensive one, but we learned a fine lesson. As in this case, everything in Korea is topsy-turvy.

The hakeme technique, which originated in Korea, was, I believe, discovered by chance when people tried to rectify crackling and flaking caused by poor adhesion between the clay body and white slip, when dipped. Crudely brushed white slip adheres to the body better. However, the brush-marks on the surface of the ware captured the eyes of the Japanese connoisseur, to be treasured and labelled Hakeme Ware.

Many Japanese potters are attracted to hakeme and get pleasure in making it. But some tend to be too artificial, lacking the freedom seen in the Korean works that were made unself-consciously. It is only in the country potteries in Japan, those making utility ware, that one finds a degree of freshness.

I like hakeme. I have tried my hand many times and I always feel defeated and give up, although I know it is not a matter of winning or losing. It is strange that every time I visit Korea and view the buildings in the countryside and the people flocking to the markets on special days and then return to Japan, I notice that my hakeme becomes much easier, although my stay in Korea had nothing to do with hakeme.

The Koreans did it because the slip flaked off when they dipped a pot in white slip. They pressed the slip into the clay with a brush—they never talked about hakeme, they did not have such a word; all they did was to make sure the white slip was sticking onto the clay. They preferred the whiter colour to the dark clay body. But the Japanese then took it up as a self-conscious technique and gave it a name. They began to make use of it as pattern, and this is where they went wrong. They even went so far in their efforts for achievement as to take the pot to a Zen master in a monastery, thinking he had no greed or self-consciousness. They had the brushstrokes put on by the Zen master and then sold the bowl for a higher price. This was indeed a disease and a mistake from the very beginning, but this is the direction in which many Japanese go. For instance, in the early pots there would be some impurities in the clay as well as small pebbles. In the firing, the surface of the pot would burst open like a raisin in a bun, leaving a big hole around the pebble. This also became appreciated by the Japanese, but instead of letting it happen naturally, when they received an order from a patron they put some pebbles into their clay. The pot would then have a higher value. This is a sort of illness—they purposefully put pebbles into highly refined clay.

Leach:

In the decade or so before the Second World War, Hamada and Yanagi produced a craft magazine called *Kōgei*. This magazine was beautifully illustrated and printed on hand-made papers from the countryside. Some of the covers had lacquered decoration, and sometimes vegetable-dyed textiles were used. Various kinds of craftsmen communicated to each other through it, and Yanagi, a philosopher, spoke to them all, expounding his philosophy of the "kingdom of beauty" and the "unknown craftsman", giving them a native way of approaching the meaning of life, the source from which arts and crafts spring. The magazine brought individual craftsmen and students into close contact with traditional work of the country, and with that of other countries, in a manner never achieved in England. In a way, the *Kōgei* magazine was a continuation of the intellectual enthusiasm of the earlier *Shirakaba* effort, adding discussion and insight to objective reporting of craft objects and techniques.

Hamada (from Kōgei, *Vol. 8, 1931):*

"Taste" and "feeling": the former is a part, the latter is the whole.

If one is observing a pot or any good article, one must be aware that "taste" is only partial viewing, while perceiving the "feeling" of an article is seeing the whole. The person who is preoccupied with good taste will respond to the details and incidentals of the object he is viewing, but is too close to see the whole object properly. The person who is concerned with feeling stands aside and allows the work to make its natural impact on him.

The same distinction also applies to the craftsman doing his work; he can consciously create tasteful things but he cannot deliberately create things with feeling. Real feeling seems to hover impartially; it is something inherent in the nature of a work. The piece achieves its beauty irrespective of the conscious aims of the maker. Usually the craftsman sets out to produce a particular effect and is pleased or displeased with the final result, depending on how near the work comes to his original intention. In fact, the essence of the true quality of the work lies somewhere else, and his conscious efforts to achieve this quality make little difference.

Good taste is a formula, and almost anyone can develop the ability to have

113

good taste or to create good taste. But it is not so with feeling, it cannot be purchased like a new coat. Therefore, criticism or appreciation by people who deal essentially in taste is of little real value to the craftsman, whereas any genuine criticism of a work's feeling gives the maker cause for serious thought.

The connoisseur, in selecting or judging work usually chooses the tasteful, safe, pleasing pieces, as viewed from the established standard. This approach is admirable as far as it goes, and the works concerned are no doubt relatively well-balanced, pleasing pieces. But I often wish that people would take a step further and apply non-established, non-accepted standards and select work that has true directness of feeling, even if it is lacking in the expected taste. I am sure the potter himself would learn a great deal from this. People have a tendency to dwell a great deal on shape, balance, pattern, line, and so on, but they fail to see, or they forget, the whole. The article produces its own effect regardless of these piecemeal distinctions.

A work with a plain surface is a beautiful thing, but intentional, deliberate plainness becomes a type of pattern. It lacks both the beauty and the depth of the truly unadorned. By contrast, there are many articles where pattern is used in such a way as to create an effect of no pattern. The pattern that is time-tested and matured harmonizes and does not fight with the piece it adorns. In spirit, this well-decorated piece is identical to the one with truly no pattern—this is the real meaning of plainness.

Traditional raku ware is an excellent example of conscious striving after profound, unadorned beauty. These pots are in reality no more than a lump of taste made through a compromise between the connoisseur and the potter. The result seldom goes beyond self-conscious rusticity. The person who perceives a work's good taste is often regarded as a fine arbiter. But to fully appreciate a work one must see beyond the conscious intention of the maker; one must try to see the essence of the piece itself. To do this you need to stand back, and allow the true feeling to have its say.

January 1, 1949

Dear Mr. Leach,

New Year's greetings. We received your letter at the beginning of December. It was the second one we had from Europe after the war. We received your first letter in December 1947, and we wrote you a letter with our news and some photos, but are afraid it did not arrive.

We are glad to hear that you are well. We are also very well. It has been exceptionally warm this winter, with no snow and frost here.

I wonder if you remember Mashiko when I was quite young. I am now nineteen years old, and I go to Mooka High School from which my two brothers graduated. I have been studying English these four years, and it seems to me to get harder and harder. I am still clumsy and cannot write well enough. This letter is the first one written by me in English to a foreigner. I am a first-year pupil of the high school. (Our school system was changed and restarted at the beginning of last April.) Can you imagine how our family has grown since then?

Kyūzo Hamada (age 80). He was in good health while you were in Japan, but now he is too old to work and has been weak. He stopped writing his "Kokoro no rokudō" (The Six Roads of the Heart). Do you remember the special map?

Shoji " (56). He has many *shirages* (white hairs) on his shining head, but he is working hard.

Kazue " (46). She has few white hairs and she is very well.

Hideko Kimura (41). She is my mother's sister. Her house in Tokyo was burned in the war and she lives with us. Her brother must have died on the field in the Philippines.

Ryūji Hamada (24). He is attending Waseda University and he is home to spend his winter vacation.

Shinsaku " (21). He is making pots and will become a potter.

Atsuya " is myself.

Hiroko " (15). She goes to Mashiko middle school, and has started to learn English. She was born while you were in Japan last time. Do you remember that you congratulated her birth by sending a telegraph "Banzai"?

Hisako " (10). She was born after you left Japan and now goes to Mashiko primary school.

Yoshio " (6). He speaks English a little (hello, how do you do, good-bye, and so on).

Now let us tell you about our pottery.

At present seven potters are working with my father. Firing of the big kiln was just done yesterday and unloading will be on the fifth of January. Many big houses were built (big studio, big house larger than the former house, big kiln which has eight chambers, another gate-house, and so on). You will be surprised to see them. I can make many pots (vases, cups, tea-pots, dishes, bowls, and so on). I will become a potter. My eldest brother cannot make pots. I don't know whether my youngest brother will become a potter or not. I wish to go to St. Ives someday to learn European techniques, and am anxious to know if you will kindly teach me.

All of your old friends are looking forward to your coming to Japan again soon.

> With kindest regards,
> Yours sincerely,
> Atsuya Hamada

Leach:

Hamada's and Yanagi's next visit to England was not until 1952. This was Hamada's third visit, and Yanagi's second. An international conference of potters and weavers (the first of its kind in the world) was held at Dartington Hall, and it was of course logical that they should be invited to represent Japan. The conference lasted about twelve days, and the conditions were perfect. The British Council had cooperated with the educationalists at Dartington, and of course the Elmhirsts gave every kind of assistance. There was an exhibition of British crafts, a superb exhibition of Mexican crafts that had been travelling throughout Europe, and a fine collection of West African textiles. We had about one hundred delegates from all continents, and naturally many of them brought examples of their work for display. All were in high spirits, and they were talking to one another, using their fingers if they did not have a common language. They were friends in a day, brought together by the common bond of love for their crafts.

Hamada's work was well known to all, since he had several exhibitions in London in the years after his departure from St. Ives in 1923. During the thirties, The Little Gallery, started by Muriel Rose for the precise purpose of showing fine crafts, had given two shows of his and kept a permanent display of his work, as well as of the finest of English potters and textile workers of that time. The collectors had begun to gravitate to this gallery, so Hamada's work, his growth and development, was always a part of the English potting scene.

Yanagi, on the other hand, was only really known through my limited writing about him, but his contribution was a very major one to the conference. His philosophy of the "unknown craftsman", the concept of mingei, had matured, and he presented several important and exciting papers on these subjects as well as explaining the Zen concept of beauty and the Tea ceremony.

Hamada chose not to use his English, but left me to translate for him as he demonstrated. He felt quite rightly that he could say more through clay than through his limited English conversation. Yanagi's creative thought was the core of our message in words, but it was the demonstrations by Hamada without words that carried and drove home the meaning—one great step towards understanding and therefore human warmth of contact.

We went on from England across the Atlantic to a series of seminars from coast to coast in North America, which had been arranged by the Society of Contemporary Arts in Washington, D.C. This was Hamada's first visit to America. All through our travels across America after the Dartington conference, it was Yanagi and Hamada and the thought that they brought from the East that held the attention of the audiences. At first questions of a technical kind were always springing to the lips of the young potters gathered at various universities and centres across America. It became an expectation that for two or three days in each place we would have to hold out against persistent technical questions, especially concerning glaze recipes, before it became apparent that there was something more than an outside-in approach. The real issues only gradually emerged. What was "the good pot"; how did beauty and truth combine in this field in a scientific and industrial epoch; what was the way for students to release their inner life into outward work, not only in America but in all industrialized countries? Here for the first time an Oriental spoke a word and another acted on it. Everywhere across the United States during those three months of seminars we received hospitality and generosity. It was a wonderful experience.

One of the highlights of the tour was at Santa Fe, New Mexico, and in the pueblos surrounding it, to which we were taken by a kind American friend who introduced us to some of the Indian peoples. At Santa Fe I feared lest we might miss meeting the American Indian potter Maria Martinez. We went to her pueblo, San Ildefonso. She was not at home, and no one knew where she was. Snow was on the ground, and we turned to go. We looked round to see if there were any signs of smoke. Sure enough, there was smoke coming from behind one of the adobe buildings, and there we found Maria Martinez, waiting for a heap of ash to cool off sufficiently to withdraw the shining black pots with a piece of iron, gradually, so that they would not crack.

Before leaving, we asked Maria if she and her son would care to come to Santa Fe for the first lecture and demonstration that we were due to give in the brand new international craft museum. There, in due course, she came and sat amongst the audience in all her finery of handspun vegetable-dyed clothing and silver ornaments set with turquoise. I had to give the introduction and translate for Yanagi; he did not feel at ease speaking English. When I had finished, I stepped off the platform and, seeing Maria and her son in the audience, went and sat next to them. Hamada seated himself cross-legged before his Japanese wheel, which had been made ready for him on the stage. Maria at my side immediately bent forward, mouth slightly ajar, watching intently. She just caught the corner of my eye, and a little bit later she put her hand on my knee gently and said, "Why didn't you tell us? Please come back. Anything you want." The barriers were down—here was the contact that I felt, and I know Hamada felt, breaking down all barriers and all the things that insert themselves between the communion of man with man. Words were hardly necessary. She had beauty in her approach to clay; there was beauty in her face, in her clothing, the best, I thought, in that whole room—the only one who belonged to that arid land.

From there we made our way to San Francisco and eventually flew to Hawaii, where we spent a fortnight en route to Tokyo. In Japan we three travelled to the branches of the Mingei Society in different parts of the country to report on that first Dartington Conference of craftsmen and the American tour.

Hamada was a potter of maturity at this time—intellect and intuition in full interplay, not seeking rarity, not even understatement for the sake of understatement, any more than an autumn leaf, but, rather, attaining balance; no longer stark, just his own true self. In retrospect, I feel that this journey of Yanagi's and Hamada's to England to represent the East was very significant. When we crossed the United States, Hamada experienced the importance of the American Indian influence. After meeting Maria Martinez, he was able to digest what he had seen—their baskets, their inherited tribal pattern making. He received a new experience, certainly confirming his previous experiences in the East. I think to both of them those adventures in the West must have brought a sense of maturing valuation, of assurance that their thought had root and meaning and was going to be listened to. They came home to travel round the country, reporting these impressions and sharing their experiences with other craftsmen of Japan.

We went right up to the northernmost area of Honshu, and then went all the way down the western coast, passing from prefecture to prefecture, with their different patterns of gathering rice, winnowing, making different haystacks, etc. We stopped at those towns where the craft movement had established museums and where there was a public wanting to hear what we had to tell of our experiences abroad. Yanagi was a very good speaker, but Hamada is in a way still more so: he is so human, so warm, so direct that people are magnetized by his vitality and truthfulness.

One example was up at the city of Matsumoto, two thousand feet above the sea in a valley sixty miles long and about fifteen miles wide. In this medieval city there is a wood-worker, Sanshirō Ikeda, whom I got to know very well. Towards the afternoon he would often come over to me and bring enlargements of my sketches—he was always asking me to make drawings of furniture and talk about the thickness of the seat, the thickness that would hold the spokes for a human type of chair, or the thickness of the leg, the curve of the back to fit the body, and so on. One day Ikeda summoned a dozen of his best men together with the furniture they had made and asked to meet us in his small factory to hear our criticism. None of us had made chairs—I had made one or two, but nothing to speak of, and Hamada was more familiar with wood than I. Hamada seized the occasion and said: "There are lots of things here that are just not quite right. It is difficult for us Japanese to know with our bodies what is right, because we were not accustomed in the old Japanese life to sitting on chairs at tables. So it is essential to try with our bodies to feel what is comfortable. How many of you use these chairs in your own houses? Will you put up your hands?" Only one did. Hamada said, "How can you expect to make good chairs?"

On another occasion at a first opening of a new branch of the Mingei Society in one of the central country towns, we spoke for about an hour and a half to a large gathering in a beautiful private merchant's house, which was being given to the local branch of the craft movement. Hamada talked very well; then, belatedly, a young Japanese journalist stood up and asked permission to speak. He said that he wrote a column in one of the leading local papers dealing with contemporary problems for the young people of that area of Japan. Nothing was said impertinently, but he thrust questions at Hamada, who was not offended but took them seriously. His theme was that many of these young people felt that Yanagi's aesthetic was old hat. "What," he said, "has it got to do with us today, in a machine age?" He was insistent, and some of the audience tried to silence him, but Hamada went on quietly for a full hour. He told the story of how we had visited Charles Eames, the famous designer of the chairs that bear his name, in Los Angeles. There we sat on Japanese tatami matting in the large open house that Eames had designed himself. We had a memorable meeting with him and his delightful wife and partner. He showed us a colour film of, of all strange things, a great variety of loaves of bread. He played with them on the screen as if they were toys with an astonishing freedom of imagination. They became alive as actors in a contemporary scene. As they could not move, he moved the camera in a creative way instead. He showed such an open acceptance of life that, in combination with his talk, all three of us received a new answer to the problem that we were seeking to solve. Here was a man with a creative, positive solution, who accepted that which was good and true from the past and the present whilst looking ahead to the future. At the end of the story the young reporter fell silent and bowed low, thanking Hamada quite humbly for having put a case that he had not previously grasped.

Eames's creative play with his "puppets" of bread on a sixteen-millimetre film told of a free and creative mind that in some respects was deeper than that of the Scandinavian designers and of the older Bauhaus movement behind them. Somehow this man had contrived to dissipate the anxieties with which most of us are beset. Like Hamada, he has created his own world. I doubt whether it is a matter for words so much as for practice. What Hamada said, broadly speaking, was that contained in Eames's approach there is an easy playfulness of mind that gives a positive assurance in the midst of what seems a mechanical world.

On the many subsequent trips that Hamada has made to America, he has always visited Eames. It has become the custom of both men on these visits to exchange toys. Hamada's stories of these visits are a pleasure to hear and are evidence of the understanding between the two men.

Hamada:

When I first met Charles Eames and had a friendly talk with him, he mentioned how he went about designing a new chair. First, he said, he had to study old chairs his grandparents used. He sat on them and found nothing wrong with them. He said he realized then that his grandparents, his parents, and he himself did not differ greatly in physique, and the old chairs were just as comfortable as new ones. He said he even thought then that the older chairs had better designs than the latest ones and that actually there were no such things as classical and modern chair designs. The chairs of today, he said, are designed with emphasis on efficiency and logic, but the old ones have the same qualities. He concluded that the only difference between the old and new is that our mode of living has changed slightly.

The Japanese words for chair, table, and Western cooking bring back old memories. The words were still new when I was young and made me feel that the great advent of Western civilization in Japan was just round the corner. But I still cannot understand the knack of chairs. This may be because chairs were never a part of my young life, with the exceptions of using them at school and perching on the edge of them in formal guest rooms.

Come to think of it, when I was a junior school student, I used to frequent the antique shops in Yokohama dealing in second-hand Western-style furniture sold by foreign residents returning home. I was fond of the shops because of the fancy and quaint-looking chairs on display. I never fancied myself buying chairs then.

In Japan today chairs are more and more in demand with the changing mode of living. The time has come for us to have eyes to know good chairs from bad.

In St. Ives, Leach and I had many fine talks over tea with Mrs. Podmore about homespun, furniture, food, and the houses of England. Many things that I vaguely understood became clear. Leach and I were deeply impressed. We returned to the pottery and started to make chairs and tables.

We were very fond of furniture and often visited auctions in the countryside, where we bought a few pieces. I learned a lot from these experiences. Of all British furniture, I am especially fond of the Windsor and the rush-bottom chairs. I always was attracted to these chairs whenever they were exhibited at museums or sold at second-hand shops.

At a shop in an alley near the National Gallery in London was a set of Windsor chairs tied in a bundle with rope. They cost thirty shillings apiece (fifteen yen then at the foreign exchange rate) but they were too expensive for me. Before leaving England, I purchased five or six hunting watches, but I could not buy the chairs because of the expensive freight charges.

Upon returning to Japan, I found that a friend was about to depart for England. I told him about the chairs, gave him the location of the shop, and asked him if he could buy me one chair. He kept his promise and brought back a Windsor chair from England. I had no house then, so I left the chair at Kawai's place. It was delightful to sit on my own chair every time I visited Kyoto.

The chair was more than two hundred years old, but in the best condition. That sturdy chair made of solid wood never made you tired, even when sitting on it for hours. And the chair made its owner very proud of possessing it. I still use the chair in Mashiko. The legs have become shorter with the years, and the size now is just right for me.

In 1929, when Yanagi and I were planning to visit England, a wealthy shop-owner friend in Kyoto, upon hearing the story of my chair, asked us to purchase a complete set of sturdy British furniture for his new house. He handed us thirty thousand yen (an enormous amount of money at that time) and asked us to select as many chairs as we could because there might be others in Japan who would want them.

We were so carried away in looking for furniture after arriving in England that we soon ran out of money. The revenues from both Kawai's and my personal exhibitions were added to the fund, but the money still was not enough. So we finally cabled to Japan and received an additional ten or twenty thousand yen. Since we wanted to purchase as many chairs as possible, we visited a trustworthy furniture dealer every Monday to choose good Windsor and rush-bottom ones from a large array of chairs. In all, we purchased more than three hundred chairs.

This request from the dealer in Kyoto was the best kind of opportunity for me to study and appreciate chairs. Buying three hundred pieces is really part of the furniture dealer's trade, but dealers handle chairs just to make money. We had to sort out good chairs on our own judgment, not for ourselves but for the sake of others who would treasure the chairs for years. It was really a difficult task, but thanks to a good friend like Yanagi, everything was possible.

Many Japanese who visit England often return home with large sets of British furniture, usually fancy and in a strongly European decorative style. But when we went looking for chairs, we never tried to pick out designs that seemed Western. As a result, we learned not only about, but *from* Western furniture. We did not do any research before we bought chairs. We first scrutinized the chairs, selected the good ones, then purchased those that appealed to both of our hearts without logic. And as a result, we learned. We did not have anything with which to measure the "goodness" or "badness" of the articles; we directly approached the chairs and simply bought the ones we thought were overwhelming.

We never purchased chairs because they matched our tastes or because they were appealing due to fancy designs. We selected those we simply thought were agreeable, sat on them, purchased the ones that were comfortable, and gradually began to love the chairs. Chairs we purchased included those made in the U.S.A., England, Spain, and Sweden. We never felt bored with the chairs we collected. Many collectors buy new chairs when they get tired of old ones, but we never had that feeling. The longer we had the chairs, the more we liked them. Instead of our minds appraising the chairs, the chairs were understood by our bodies.

Thus, through these contacts with old furniture, we came to the conclusion that British chairs are the best, being sturdy, less decorative, used for generations, made of good woods and with natural elbow grease. Maybe because I was constantly in touch with sturdy British furniture from the beginning, I frankly do not trust the good-design products. Old British Windsor chairs have better designs than anyone today can create. Such furniture has been subject to people's use and critical eyes for generations; therefore, the designs are seasoned to satisfy the tastes of all during the long course of history. Only chosen items survived the rigours of history in construction and design.

In High Wycombe near Windsor, I once saw a bearded old man in a nearby forest making a Windsor chair. He was working on the curved back of the chair. At intervals he stepped into the forest and returned with a piece of wood he thought appropriate, placed the wood over a fire, and bent it. He had a lot of failures, which immediately became firewood. I thought this was a true close-up picture of a man really at work.

A few years ago I visited a village in Spain where simple chairs are made, watched the people at work, and was strongly impressed. It took a seasoned worker only fifteen minutes to shape a limb and have it ready for the structural assembly work.

It is also a wonder that the chairs of the colonial period in America are so simple in design yet elaborately made and lighter than the British counterparts. This was something I could not understand. Anyone would think that the early settlers in the New World would make things roughly and unskilfully. But, on the contrary, the British, French, Spanish, Dutch, and German methods were all incorporated in American life and resulted in the production of lighter and intricate chairs. Come to think of it, the chairs of the early American days can be regarded as modernized versions of the old British chairs. The American chairs often are not made of oak or hardwood, but of cheap pine.

The furniture of the American Shakers especially has good features we can learn from. These simple chairs are bright and light in construction, finish, and colour, completely divorced from intellectual coldness and excessive decoration.

Furniture that creates trends or fashion should always bear good elements that allow it to be treasured when the design becomes classic with the disappearance of the fashion. It is a pity that furniture makers today merely follow fashion, are interested only in selling their products, and overlook the basic rules of furniture making.

People of today are liable to trust what the computers say and are carried away by anything new. But old and new are just the opposite sides of a single sheet of paper.

Leach:

The period of change when a country industrializes and work becomes much more turned over to the machine and to scientific leadership, at the expense of the use of the human heart and hand, gave birth to parallel movements on two sides of our globe. The first, in England, was due to William Morris. Three-quarters of a century later Sōetsu Yanagi started his movement in Japan. The early days of the latter were contemporaneous with the Bauhaus movement in Germany, but that was an attempt to humanize industrialization of labour by acceptance of materialism, or, let us say, of intellect over intuition and a rejection of Victorian fantasy.

In 1952, we brought to England and the U.S. Yanagi's ideas and Hamada's practice. This was only a passing encounter for the West, perhaps, but the response indicated that seeds were sown. I do know that one product of the agony of the decade of the sixties in the West seems to be a new, intense, grass-roots interest and activity in handwork that may bear substantial fruit, if new leaders with vision arise.

We then went on to Japan, to a country still confused and searching in the aftermath of a decade or more of nationalism, war, and its terrible isolation, to give the great news about the reception of Yanagi's Oriental thought in the West and to provide a long-needed stimulus from abroad with a travelling exhibition of Western folkcrafts my Japanese friends had purchased. This trip throughout Japan was one of the climaxes of Yanagi's long-term aim of giving encouragement to and exhorting people to preserve their traditions and work. The exhibit of Western folkcrafts provided a reference for the Japanese craftsmen and the public to see, compare, and evaluate their native work. Hardship and deprivation make inescapable demands, and a sudden explosion of economic prosperity results in equally foreseeable trends. The most sought-after books during the American occupation of Japan were American mail-order clothing catalogues, and the country's delight in, or acceptance of, plastic and neon has increased as her industry and trade "hegemony" has grown.

Japan is losing her old customs and is becoming international in thought and action. It is in this new life of international travel and exchange that we have to find a way of truth in the change-over. This is a great and long experiment, and the artist has the responsibility of providing the objects that will enhance the life of his society. A stage has to be passed through of making all sorts of mistakes in order to reach a true answer.

Hamada:

To return to what I said before about mingei, the problem is how does the individual artist today approach folkcraft. Of course the answer is that he should look after his character first. The problem of his own character must come foremost.

With one's intellect, with one's mind, one can understand what tradition means. The folk art formula may be fed through the mind and through the intellect. But in work, what comes out must come out through one's own finger-tips, one's own hands, otherwise it is no work at all.

Craftsmen themselves today must begin to change in this direction. But change for its own sake is no good. Just because there is a need for change, looking for ways of changing, for change's sake only, will never do. If an artist has a tight hold on himself, then what is important also is for him to be able to loosen himself. It is no use if somebody tightens you and then someone comes to help loosen you. Outside help will only ruin your work.

Worse than that are those people who do not have any hold on themselves at all. Also there are those who have such a tight hold on themselves that they do not know how to loosen. There should now be a very good creative critic who is able to put all these thoughts together and verbalize them, but there are few who are able to associate with mingei at its real depth. To meet people of depth is a rare thing in any area.

There are three interlinked terms that are the core of the mingei movement—health, naturalness, and beauty. These are three aspects or attributes of objects made by correctly following or going along with natural forces. Because Yanagi was a critic and dealt with words, he used the term "beauty" a great deal to express what he was trying to say. In my case, being a workman, I do not feel any lack by not using that word. It is the experience—how the experience is accepted—that is important, not the word. It is rather dangerous for a maker or producer of objects to use that word beauty. Perhaps in my early days I may have used it, but these days never.

Beauty is not in the head or the heart, but in the abdomen. One cannot verbalize it; it is beyond verbalization. If it is solidified and produced as an object, then it is real. Once you understand that, the word beauty becomes superficial and not worthy of attention. Yanagi, too, in spite of the fact that he used the word beauty, realized that there should be a measuring tape without marks on it and used such terms to try to express this.

People use the same words—beauty, for instance—but the meanings change with the person. But when one makes things, it has one and the same meaning, not limited to shape or form or outer appearance. To use such terms as beauty has nothing to do with what happens, the inner experience. In the mingei group, many people go around using the word beauty, but quite often one finds that these people do not have any understanding whatever of how normal beauty is.

Many criticize Kawai for having moved away from folk art, but actually that is not so. He really understood mingei because he did not go away from the central point. There is a strength in Kawai's work and a bit of weakness as well. If he did not go to extremes, he was not satisfied. This was his weakness, and he knew it very well. It would have been wrong for Kawai to try to become a country potter. By understanding mingei, people can still do what is right for them to do, within themselves. Kawai stayed as he was, did not try to become a folk potter. Tomimoto also developed himself as he was.

The three terms that are the core of mingei—health, naturalness, and beauty —are the core around which all of my friends developed. This is true mingei from my point of view; this is the definition of mingei. All of my friends, including Kawai, knew this from the inside and therefore never actually moved away from it. Not only that, they went on to develop individually without colliding with each other.

The example of the crane coming down from his nest to stay awhile and then returning alone is important in the sense that I am trying to explain the role of the individual artist. It looks as if such people have left the mingei concept, but they have eaten, they have remained. They are not stagnant; they remain in mingei and yet are trying to develop themselves from mingei. This is what I am trying to say, using Kawai as an example. People such as Kawai and Tomimoto have trodden their true path, they have eaten folkcrafts and then have developed their own path. This is legitimate, the natural thing, for them. Kawai was weak physically and therefore he developed his intellect more.

Kawai called himself a son of an overly wealthy family and wanted to disown himself from any riches that might spoil him. He considered that such freedom allowed him to do what he wanted. But he should not have thought of himself; such things ought not to have bothered him—whether he was or was not rich, he should have been free.

I feel myself a contrast to Kawai. The reason why I am bringing in Kawai so much is because we contrasted so strongly.

Whenever I encountered my friends and their work—anything, whether people or things—I reflected myself against that particular thing and made myself master it if I happened to feel defeated. If I could not live up to the standard of what I was encountering, I urged myself to try to meet that standard, to overcome it, to leave behind my past and go forward. People and objects were mentors for me. Not as people or finished products, but everything I encountered was an example against which I reflected—a mirror.

I have not come alone to where I am now. It is due to the fact that there were people around me who were first-rate. Because they were first-rate, I feel I have come as far as I have, and this point is essential.

Leach:

I recall Hamada telling a famous story of Priest Hakuin, the Zen priest who also was a painter. A girl gave birth to an illegitimate child. The father was Hakuin, so rumour had it. Upon being confronted with this, Hakuin said, "Indeed", and departed from the village. Many years later he returned. The people who remembered him stopped, amazed, and said, "So you were not the father of the child after all." "Indeed," said the priest.

There is another Zen story, a famous one, about crossing the river. It was flooding and there was a young girl who could not get across to the other side· The only people present were a Zen monk accompanied by another young monk. The senior monk carried this girl across the river and left her there, and they went on their way. Shortly afterwards the young monk could not contain himself any longer and confronted his companion. "You are a Zen monk, a priest. How could you touch a female like that and behave in such a manner. It's sacrilege." Or some words to that effect. Then the first monk said to the younger, "Are you still carrying her?"

Hamada was in the very midst of his life pattern, doing the middle work of his life. What had seemed stark to me when I first went to Japan and saw his earlier work all made with the rough clay and materials of Mashiko had now matured into something that I think owes its root to an added depth. His work had austerity, nobility, simpleness, warmth, and naturalness, at one and the same time. The virtue of Hamada's pots are the innate virtues of the man himself, as they must be in any good artist's work. His pots are warm, generous, spontaneous, and sturdy; they are as of the earth, earthy, and his main decorations are redolent of his immediate countryside—of the grass, grassy, of the brush, brush-like. His pots articulate like an oak tree, the bones of structure are not concealed, the modulations of form are intuitive, and all his pots stand firm on their feet. If his pots take you with a sense of surprise, it is because he himself is ready to be taken by surprise. This is far removed from setting out to take his audience by storm. He still uses the limited traditional Mashiko glaze materials and he obtains a variety and quality by playing them one over another, often perhaps with wax resist patterns between. It is difficult to follow the exact process, even for a fellow potter. The originality is hidden behind the most direct and ordinary and it is born not of theory but from constant practice and close familiarity with his tools and materials, with nature behind it all.

Hamada:

In Mashiko the potters obtained clay and kiln materials from nearby, and wood from the local forest. Ash and stone for glazes were available in the neighbourhood. Kaki glaze, which is used most, is made from the powder of stone quarried in the neighbouring village; iron powder came from iron dust at the blacksmith's; copper powder from old copper pans, and even brushes from the hair of local dogs. These materials are never first-class. Yet, here is purity and harmony as seen in Japanese paper, brush, and ink, instead of foreign paper and fountain pen. And here survived local life that could maintain the quality of this work. Most of the people here were half-farmers and half-potters. Each family had a big workshop and one to three climbing kilns, and all family members worked there. Even when I moved there, these potteries were becoming outdated and washed away in the waves of progress. However, today still they retain a sort of comfort compared with the people in Seto and other industrial pottery areas, who work much harder.

I did not choose to use my technical training when I went to Mashiko. I did not need it. My work materialized by merely adjusting myself to the conditions there.

I have used the clay and glazes of Mashiko and have never given up the objective of making first-class work from impure, lower-rated natural materials. I thought it was much better than doing second- or third-class work with top-rated, chemically purer materials.

My glazes are not actually first class, but I sometimes think they are, depending upon the way I use them. I have come to think that the glazes are becoming my own personal possessions instead of borrowed things.

I manage to get along with only five or six glazes. I use them over and under each other, sometimes with ochre slip, which produces many colour variations. If I count all the variations, the number and types of glazes are countless. It is just like a Persian carpet made up of six different colours.

When I visit a potter's workshop, I normally observe a variety of experimental glazes of different formulas flooding the shelves. I am different. I prefer only a limited number of glazes, mixed in large quantities. I like to work out of a big vat. In this manner I can dip the whole pot in the glaze. If it is too large for my vat, I use a ladle and pour the glaze over it. Without a large quantity, it is impossible to apply the glaze in a vivid and lively manner.

Perhaps someday I will use celadons, copper-reds, etc., but at present I am too busy with my own glazes. The slight, subtle tone variations possible in my glazes keep me occupied.

In addition to a clay body, if you have volcanic or feldspathic stone, or a type of china clay and ash for glaze, you can make pottery. We must not allow ourselves to complain of the lack of variety or quality of materials. Instead we must learn how to make full use of given natural materials and processes. Fine white porcelain, celadon, or tenmoku were made just because such materials were available in that area without spending any special effort. Clay, form, and glaze were perfectly integrated. But later copies of these pots made in other countries have a cold, empty, calculated feeling no matter how technically competent the potter is. This fact is so plain that very skilful potters often fail to recognize it. Strange to say, potters who excel in copying are often not so good at creating their own works, perhaps because these people do not become themselves as they pursue the glazes of others.

Out of two materials you can make a nice glaze. Take a finely ground volcanic or feldspathic stone. Add 20 percent black wood ash (not burned sufficiently to make it gray or white) for your first test. Many mixtures of finely ground stone and clays will melt if they are fluxed by the addition of ash. It is simple to test how to use the raw materials of one's own area. First, experiment with ash and stone in eleven combinations. The first experiment will be no ash, and stone only; the second will be one part ash and nine parts stone; third, two parts ash and eight parts stone, and so on to the eleventh experiment, ash alone. The type of ash used plus the iron content of the stone will produce many variations. The same tests should be made with clay and ash. When testing dry materials, I weigh them on scales, but if they are liquid, I mix them by estimating the quantities.

I would fire these different glaze tests to a temperature varying between 1,250° and 1,300° C. There will be a slight difference in the specific gravities between those measured on a scale and mixed from liquids, but it does not matter which method is used provided you get interesting glazes from the tests.

In my second testings I would make minor adjustments in the proportions, evolving the combinations that appear most interesting. This is the most practical way of experimenting.

However, I am aware that many experienced and skilful potters do not favour this idea of narrowing the targets one by one. They prefer to aim at once for the bull's-eye, and I have witnessed that sometimes they hit it.

The standard transparent glaze of Mashiko is produced from a stone called *terayama* from Yaita in the northern part of the prefecture. It is a stone, not a true feldspar; its silica content is very high. It is finely ground and mixed with an equal quantity of washed and sieved wood ash.

And now about the ash. In olden days, small pieces of firewood and branches were used as fuel in homes. This produced a very consistent quality of ash: slender branches rather than the large trunks of the tree produce the best ash. Bark and leaves also produce good ash. The completely burned ash turns yellow with age due to the alkaline content. If you can wait until this change, you get the best ash. This you cannot ask someone else to do. The hardened ashes should be left at the bottom of your hearth for a long time. Cardboard and newspaper should not be used, because their ash is unsatisfactory for glaze. We always start our fires with twigs instead of newspaper for this reason. Ash from soft wood such as pine makes glaze of soft tone, and that from hard wood such as oak and chestnut makes a hard-toned glaze. Ash from rushes and straw is harder than that of wood. We do not use bamboo in our fire-place because bamboo ash is almost pure silica and when mixed with wood ash raises the melting point. Also, rice, wheat, and reeds produce high silica ash. The fire-place ash is the basis for our transparent glaze, but when high silica ash is added, the glaze becomes more opaque. Ash of varying types should be carefully sorted and stored for specific uses.

Rice husk (nuka) ash makes a white glaze, but wheat or barley husk ash makes a yellowish glaze. The difference between wheat and rice is very strange. There are two types of rice in Japan, a glutinous rice and our ordinary rice, and there is also a difference in their ash. I do not know why, but the chaff ash of non-glutinous rice is light and smooth, while that of the glutinous rice is sticky. Farmers mix the two together for fertilizer, but we must make a rigid distinction between them.

The proper handling of ash is troublesome but extremely important. How the two kinds of rice maintain their characteristics to the end, even when they are reduced to ash and fired to the temperature of 1,300° C. is really amazing—something out of nature that cannot be understood. Maybe we should leave the mystery as a mystery; it is no use trying to analyze it and understand it; rather than waste time on that, make something beautiful.

Such analysis was exactly what the ceramic testing institute was trying to do. We would all go wrong if we tried to analyse to the nth degree. This point is very important for young potters to understand—not to get caught up in the theory but to realize there is value in fairy tales, in fantasy, in fiction. Each material that is produced by nature, even when fired to a high temperature, 1,300° C., still maintains its own personal identity. This is a miracle that we should leave alone and not try to pick apart with our intellect. Leave the mystery a mystery, just as Mr. Uno, the Kyoto man who came visiting the institute and teased us about weighing everything, said, "I can make better glaze with my instinct." He combined his materials by eye and made a very good glaze, which proved his point. Testing and weighing chemically pure materials is like a very large and complicated target at first, but even if one gets to hit the exact centre of the bull's-eye every time it will not answer anything.

The opaque white glazes made from rice straw ash or from rice nuka ash are highly prized among potters in America. When I was teaching and demonstrating at a university in California, I asked the potters to bring rice straw ash if they wished to learn the method of producing this white glaze. On the following day they brought the ash, and I instructed them to grind it in a pestle and mortar, wash it over and over with water, and finally dry it. I told the potters to forget their scales, to make the glaze by putting in thumb and forefinger pinches of ash and nothing could go wrong. They were very startled. We glazed pots with this glaze and fired them in their gas kiln. The long-admired white glaze, said to be derived in the Sung dynasty, was reproduced. That this highly desired glaze could be a product of ash measured by a few finger pinches rather shocked the group. On the other hand, they showed the highest respect for me, and made my job of teaching much easier from then on.

The manner of making natural glazes is generally done by combining a powdered stone that fuses in the kiln with clay and ash in varying proportions. By varying the proportions of all three materials you will get a large variety of glazes. Then vary the materials, a different stone, a different clay, and a different ash. There is no end to the glazes you will get. As you discover the many shades and different glaze colours, you will come to know the nature of the materials at hand. This is the best way to try. Even an amateur can understand if it is done like this. Try from the impossible to the impossible. It is a great joy and great fun to experiment in this way. It is actually very scientific and not the hit-and-miss kind of thing it appears to be. Then make an analysis of what you have done.

Kaki glaze (persimmon red) is one of the traditional Mashiko glazes used on the standard kitchen ware. It is made from a soft stone used for building, and I was told that the glaze was discovered by accident years ago. The stone, which is rather refractory, was used to close up the kiln doors in place of fire bricks, which were not available in sufficient quantity. On opening the kiln, the surface exposed to the heat and fire was found to be a perfect kaki glaze. We only mix the powdered stone with water to obtain this kaki glaze. By adding 20 percent wood ash a wonderful tenmoku is obtained, and sometimes I pour the kaki over the tenmoku for an interesting effect. If I add more ash (about 40 percent) or transparent glaze to the kaki, it makes ame, a greenish brown, slightly transparent, syrupy glaze.

For the white, almost opaque glaze; we mix equal parts of *terayama* stone, wood ash, and rice straw or nuka ash. If the iron content of the body is high, the glaze will become blue-grey. I often dip the raw pot in a thin ochre slip as a base for this glaze and also for the tenmoku glaze.

For green glaze; 5 percent copper oxide is added to the white glaze.

For clear glaze: we use a greater quantity of wood ash.

For iron rust glaze: water is simply added to ground volcanic sandstone.

For tenmoku: we add 20 percent wood ash to kaki.

For iron brown glaze: we add about 40 percent wood ash to kaki.

Kaki glaze over transparent glaze with a wax resist pattern between produces an interesting effect.

The above are all the glazes we use at Mashiko, although, of course, they can be varied in innumerable combinations. For example, black and rice-nuka-ash white glaze may be poured over a pot that had been dipped in ochre slip before biscuiting. The black glaze may be trailed or splashed over white opaque glaze, each half of a pot may be dipped separately in white translucent and black glaze, a finger-wipe design may be made immediately after dipping in black glaze, or iron rust may be poured or trailed over black glaze.

By varying the thickness of the glaze, the method of application (pouring, trailing, splashing, dipping, or brushing), it is possible to produce almost endless variations from my six glazes.

Although many other pigments are available, most of my work is done with iron. My experience shows that the iron flakes produced at the blacksmith shop are the best. These are finely ground and mixed with an equal part of slip. This gives me a very dark brown-black for painting over transparent glaze immediately after the glaze has been applied. I also mix equal parts of tenmoku glaze and transparent glaze for a brown pigment for on-glaze painting. I find these two mixes congenial to the rest of my materials, and in the many years I have been potting, I have not required any more.

My pigments combined with slip are very thick, and it is necessary to use a brush with long, floppy bristles in decorating pots. The brush must hold a generous amount of heavy liquid. Following the old Mashiko practice, I make my own brushes from the long, coarse hair at the back of a dog's neck. The fine, shorter hair is removed, the remaining hair bound with thread, inserted in a piece of split bamboo, and bound again. People with knowledge of good Japanese brushes always say that our dog hair brush is very bad because paints tend to flow off in one stroke, but it is a good brush for potters, since we use thick liquids. This brush is good for any kind of thick pigments: lines are easily extended; thick and thin lines can be drawn; and it has an amazingly long life, even when used against the rough surface of clay materials. When painting designs on greenware or rough biscuit surfaces, the tip of an ordinary brush would soon fray and wear out. But I have been using my brush for more than ten years. The long-lasting secret is that when the paint drops off from the tip of my brush, I just pull it along to draw the design. This is a good technique to avoid ruining the brush.

One decorating technique I enjoy is wax resist. I melt paraffin wax and then add double the amount of paraffin oil (kerosene). When the pot is decorated with a waxed pattern, the waxed area is kept free of pigment or glaze. Thus, the design is revealed when the wax melts in the firing. Sometimes I use wax directly on the biscuited body. At other times, I apply a wax brush design after the first glaze coat, before the pot is dipped in a second glaze, or before a final iron pigment brushing. A painted pattern of iron brush-work on the glaze may also be covered with wax before the pot is brushed with iron or dipped into a second glaze. Sometimes a glaze trail pattern over a primary glaze is waxed before the pot is dipped in a second glaze. Still another method is to paint with wax on greenware and dip the pot in thin ochre slip before the biscuit firing. When I am glazing this pot I can see where my slip pattern is under the glaze, because the absorption is different. I can then brush an iron pigment pattern in the area I want.

I have been making pots with salt glaze since my American trip in 1952. My experimentation with salt was a filler until I felt I was ready to start raku. At the beginning, all my salt pots appeared rather Western, to my surprise. But after many years, I feel my salt-glazed pots have mostly become Japanese. The method is originally German, the clay is Mashiko, and the salt is an imported coarse salt from Spain. The proper rock salt is unobtainable due to limits on imports. My smallest kiln is now used for salt glaze firing. For salt glaze, greenware is brushed or decorated with such pigments as iron, manganese, or cobalt, mixed with a little slip or glaze. I use small shells reinforced with clay underneath as stilts. Because the shell is pure lime and it withstands strong fire, the bottoms of the pieces do not stick to the shelf and are thoroughly glazed underneath.

It was interesting to discover that cobalt, which I had not used before because of its harshness, becomes very subdued with salt glaze. I have, therefore, used it often in salt glaze firing.

There are many hazards in doing salt glaze, for salt will attack the bricks of the kiln itself, causing material from the ceiling of the kiln to drop down on the pots. Salt sometimes penetrates the body and causes bottles to bend and stick to one another. However, it is because the risks are great that I have found great stimulation in using this technique. After over sixty years of making pottery, one can become too comfortable and proficient. It is the very challenge of this direct, primitive method, with all its possibilities for failure, that has proved an exhilarating experience for me.

The large kiln has eight chambers and fires eight thousand pieces; the medium kiln has five chambers for two thousand pots. I built a two-chamber salt kiln that fires about two hundred pots. Each chamber has a back row of permanent shelves, in front of which tiers of saggers are set up. The larger pots are placed on shelves or on top of the bungs of saggers.

It takes about four days to fire the large kiln, two days for the medium kiln, which I now fire most often, and one day for the salt kiln. We fire to 1,300° C. We judge the temperature by the colour of the flame and the brilliance we can see in the chamber. We never use pyrometers or cones, but sometimes we take out test rings, mainly in the salt kiln.

The firewood is red pine. I find the wood of this pine, trees between thirty and forty years old, to be the best firing fuel, because the flame it produces is soft, long-lasting, and clean. It is best to cut the trees in December or January, when there is less sap. The Japanese black pine produces a strong fire, but the flame is short and severe, so I do not recommend it. When observing the mountains in the distance during tea time, I engage in a monologue over tea and cakes: "That mountain over there in two years will begin to produce good firewood." Through this kind of monologue, repeated for many years, one comes to understand which types of wood are good and which are bad for kiln firing.

Leach:

Hamada's whole coterie of buildings has become something like a compound, nestled against a hillside above the level of the watery rice fields that lie between Hamada's home and the town. Two sons, Shinsaku and Atsuya, work with their father; there are two other workers, Masao and Uma-san, who have worked years with him; and often one or two students are there for periods of study. The relationship of the workshop to the master, of the workers to their head, their leader, is something that we in the West have to look abroad to rediscover and appreciate. We, starting after art school training, have lost our long centuries of continuous experience of the best way of making things in workshop companionship. In Japan there was rootage, and in craft the long, deep tap root is very important. Hamada's workshops are quiet, everybody is skilled in his contribution, has pride in his work, in keeping the workshops in order. Everyone may go on working deep into the night, although exhausted, in order to make sure of getting the last pot into that great kiln so that the pieces will be ready for their annual show in Tokyo. That kind of quiet relationship and the respectfulness and trust in the leader, the ability to work together as a group, is something that I think we in the West have almost entirely lost. Hamada's inner force produces these conditions, which can also be seen in his home and even in the harmony pervading the thousands of objects in his folk art collection, this collection that sustains him and to which he tirelessly adds.

Hamada:

Without a good eye you cannot do anything. This applies not only to the critic but also to the maker of things. In fact, a good eye is much more important than people think; most people consider it only in a vague way. At this point in my life, I think what to see and how to see it is foremost in importance.

A few years ago Shiko Munakata brought one of his calligraphy scrolls with the characters reading *Mujinzō*, meaning "Endless Collection" or "Bottomless Storehouse". *Mujin* means "without limit", and *zō* means either "collection" or "storehouse".

The scroll was meant to hang in the *tokonoma* alcove in a room of the large old farmhouse where I keep my collection of chairs, furniture, and folkcrafts from around the world that I have been collecting for fifty years. All who came to see the place admired Munakata's writing very much. But, on the other hand, I answered Munakata, "That is nonsense. It is not an endless collection. What I have here is a remnant, only a shell." In other words, nothing left is what is here, not an endless collection. In fact, the combination of Chinese characters *mu, jin,* and *zō* may also be interpreted as "Nothingness" or "Collection of Nothingness". All is empty—nothing is left. I have eaten all the good parts, the kernel. What is here is only the remains of what I have eaten. I told Munakata that his calligraphy was very fine, but what it said—*Mujinzō*—was, after all, itself still only form. "You must see where there is no form. I have eaten all the form. What is left is just empty clothing." And clothing is unimportant.

But at the same time clothing is important. It is because I have nourished myself on these objects that I can walk on further and deepen myself. But if I become lazy, drop my guard, or become careless, I shall need this clothing, these objects, again.

I was sustained and nourished by them and I am very grateful to these objects. I want to keep them—they watch me, they watch over me in my work. The things in my collection make sure that I do not lower my standards; they will warn me of any back-sliding in my work—another reason why I am grateful to them and want to preserve them. But this is for my own sake; I always do things for myself, not necessarily for others.

A collector's ultimate aim is to gather things, but our work begins by digesting a thing. Good collectors can go about without any tools or materials and be recognized by their sharp eyes. Their eyes, how they look and what they find, give things fresh meaning and beauty. I call such people true creative critics.

Yanagi was such a man. Kawai, when referring to Yanagi, always said, "Yanagi walked where there were no paths and always left a wide open road behind him." Yanagi frequently told me his dream was to encounter an item with a beauty immeasurable by any conventional yardstick.

Nearly all collectors seek value by gathering a complete set or discovering a rare piece. But these things do not interest me. I am most attracted to objects that directly move my heart or that are far beyond me.

I now know that what I was doing was right and that my eyes were right. No matter in what country or in what antique shops, I rely on my eyes. Yet I do not like to use the word beauty. Things correctly made, rightly made, properly made, and healthy—these are the ingredients of beauty. Even when going to an unfamiliar country, if such things are solidly ingrained in you, you do not go wrong. They have become part of you, and everything that is part of you goes directly into your potting.

For me the fight is over now; I have what I want. But still when I see anything that speaks to me or is beyond me, I get excited. The item may be lopsided, cracked, and unappealing to the casual observer—it makes no difference. I am most pleased when the item is new, not an antique, and cheap. It is quite encouraging to know that good things are being made today, and it is irrelevant whether or not the piece I treasure is expensive. Most of the objects in my collection, my museum, are traditional old folkcrafts, but the collection is designed to help visitors and artists prepare for the future, not create nostalgia for the past.

I have often considered the idea of opening an exhibition of new works in which artists and appreciators would work together in selecting articles for display. I think users—not just consumers—of things should also be regarded as creative artists and that their contribution should be recognized. The use of things can be a creative activity.

Leach:

Mrs. Hamada has stood by her husband all these years with girls who were proud to come and work with her and help to get their training for marriage. That household is full of that same extended cooperative feeling of warmth; for instance, the pride in providing the water for the daily bath at just the right temperature, the call of the maid who was seeing to the wood outside the bathroom to ensure the water was neither too hot nor too cold for the bather. Whilst sitting in a great cauldron within, one hears the crackle of burning wood underneath.

Hamada would get up at five in the morning and work until eight, when he had breakfast and read the newspaper. Then during the day he would work and perhaps see fifty or so visitors. When one day I expostulated with him over this he said, "If you refuse, you never know for certain whom you may have turned away." At the end of the day he would like to take a bath and, with his youngest child, or grandchild, you would hear peals of laughter and splashing water coming from the bathroom. His warm spirit pervaded the whole household. Recently the number of visitors has increased far beyond their ability to cope. Yet Hamada remains open to need, but must turn away the idly curious. He has been forced to close his gate on Sundays.

It must have been 1953 when I had a spell of making pots at Mashiko. On subsequent visits also I had the opportunity of seeing that co-operative spirit work whilst packing kilns, to see the proper inheritance of how that kind of communal work was done. And it is simply amazing. Hamada would be quietly in the centre of things, either painting or sitting with pots brought for him to decorate.

One day he told us at breakfast that there were four hundred pots, many of which were large, waiting for him to decorate and glaze. They all had to be done by four o'clock so that we could take a car to the station twelve miles away in order to be in time for a seven o'clock dinner party in Tokyo (two hours away by train). I was simply dumbfounded. How could a man possibly sit calmly and decorate and glaze such a number of pieces, even with assistants with the glazes and the brushes, the wax for resist, and so forth, sitting round him ready to help at every move? How could he think of where those pots were to go in the kiln, at what temperature, in what atmosphere, and retain in his memory what decoration he had intended to go on a shape made perhaps two months earlier? Janet and I both asked if we might watch without any interference, and he agreed. We took up our positions leaning against posts or walls. The glazes flowed onto the pots; the pieces flowed into the kiln. Seven people worked around Hamada, handing him pots to glaze and taking them away when finished, anticipating Hamada's needs or following his calm directions smoothly. Half-way through the morning we stopped for a break with green tea and salty rice biscuits, and I asked him how he did it. He replied, "I simply look at the pot and ask it what it wants." I was taken aback. I had always planned a good deal of what I did and very seldom left much to pure spontaneity. He left his pots to his intuition to take charge. Thus he avoided confusion, anxiety, all the nervous strain of the Westerner. All four hundred pots were finished in time to get in the car and catch the train. It was totally intuitive; there was no stopping for intellection. Janet tells the story of the centipede, which, when asked which leg he puts down first, was then unable to walk.

Hamada:
I feel now at my age my pots are better than when I was younger. Throwing, painting, pattern, all these techniques are quite natural to me, and I can use them at will. Before, when I tried a new pattern, I was not always happy with it. Now I am quite happy with whatever comes out as pattern; I do not have to struggle. I am so busy, meaning that there is no room for me to think about where the next pattern is going to come from. It is probably from nature that I derive the patterns. While I am painting the patterns there are usually two or three people waiting to talk to me. This means I have to proceed to the next design without stopping; there is no time for me to ponder over what to do about the next decoration. My highly trained assistants help by dipping the pots in glaze and passing them to me at the right angle and at the right time. They take them away and wash the feet, etc. I am so busy these days, it is only possible for me to work at the wheel before breakfast and after supper. In addition, there is no time for me to ponder at leisure while throwing, decorating, and glazing to fulfill my exhibition commitments. But being busy sometimes brings about

good results. For example, I have thought many times: "Why didn't I notice this before!" I am so accustomed to being busy, I feel many times that the brush, instead of my hand, is doing the painting. And strangely enough, there are scarcely any failures. Potters usually say that when you are not feeling well, you do not produce a very good thing, and if you are feeling well, you produce a thing well. One day my friend Iseki said, "Well, if you think that's true then bring me what you produced when you didn't feel well, and what you produced when you did feel well. Surely there will be no difference at all." I found he was right.

This very busy life I lead these days is helpful to me; it is one of the factors that helps me most. After throwing or decorating hurriedly before catching a train or seeing visitors, I reflect back and find the results are satisfying.

I think I have arrived at a very interesting juncture in life. I speak of this objectively. I look at my own life and say, "What an interesting point I have arrived at. I didn't expect at all that I should arrive at such a place." As long as I work I am all right; work is the best thing. In work, all these problems of formulas and individual artistry and so on disappear. That is why, however late it is, even after dinner, I always like to go off to my workshop, even if it is eight or nine in the evening, and then work on until midnight. In the mornings I begin work before breakfast about five or five-thirty; eight o'clock is my breakfast time.

The way I work when I am very busy is interesting. This morning I had to decorate pots for salt glazing before going to Tokyo. I was up working at five o'clock, and as I went about it, I asked myself a question—I gave myself a problem and I answered the problem. I already know how to work with my body, but not so much with my mind. So I again posed the question of intellect and intuition. What I did this morning is an example of what I mean by body. I had a round pot in front of me for salt glaze. The next thing I found myself doing was dipping my brush in wax and I just went bom, bom, bom, all over the pot. I then used cobalt and brushed alternately between the spaces where I had not put wax. Following that I used manganese and filled in those areas that were still empty. It was a very interesting effect without my having ever thought of it. It never occurred to me before to do such a thing, but it happened. I think I should have thought of this many, many years ago, but it just occurred to me then. It was not from my mind that it came but from my whole body; it emerged out of my middle, my lower abdomen. I have such a good feeling about having done this pot, though I have not yet seen the fired result. But I know, I can feel it, it feels good.

I hardly know what fatigue means; like this morning, for three hours I was solidly at decorating my salt glaze pots, but I did not have to look at my watch; I did not have to feel hurried, I was perfectly comfortable with myself in all the processes, and I accomplished what I intended. Even the large plates were done. As I am working, I can see things getting better and better as I go on. I get into a rhythm and it carries me.

Leach once said that he wanted to see me trail glazes on my large, two-foot dishes. I dipped out about half a ladleful of glaze. For straight lines I start to pour about one foot away from the edge of the platter opposite me. As much as possible, I avoid thinking and pull the ladle towards me in one stroke. Pouring sideways is difficult, so I turn the platter ninety degrees and trail glaze in the same manner again.

Managing diagonal, thick, and thin lines when trailing a spiral is a little difficult and needs practice. Leach confessed that such extravagant use of ash glaze is very difficult in England.

It actually does not take more than fifteen seconds to decorate and glaze one of these big dishes with poured glaze, and many visitors ask me questions: isn't that too fast; am I always satisfied; and why are they so expensive if they only take me fifteen seconds to decorate? I reply, "The dishes take me sixty years and fifteen seconds to do."

This work does not come out of my thought; rather I simply permit the movement that my hands have learned over many years. In fact, in the work forged by my body during sixty years, there is an unconscious revelation. I sense the work has become more comfortable.

For the reasons I have mentioned, my methods are getting simpler. But I have had times in the past when I wanted to try out everything, like participating in all kinds of sports whether I could do them or not. New costumes have attracted me many times and lured me to try my hand, and I trembled with joy and tested myself. But to my regret, I usually was not satisfied with the results of such new attempts. I now hope that, rather than made things, born things will increase in my work.

Leach:

I think Hamada himself has said that it was after seventy that he began to feel mature. Perhaps that is because, as one gets older, details close at hand that are not yet assessed give way to clearer perspectives of things in the middle distance and, especially, the greater distance. This is true both of memory and perception. Young people gobble up the grass all around them; I recollect that when he was twenty-eight at St. Ives he said more than once, "I shall not be able to lose my tail before I reach forty." What was he, that early Hamada, in comparison? That clear, firm handwriting has broadened now; it has become more easy, more mature. Hamada, in his life, has expanded without stopping; with the alchemy that accompanies the passage of years—wisdom, shall we say—older people develop a longer reach and ability to choose their nourishment. Yet Hamada seems to have had uncommon perception as a youth and has allowed no barriers to upset his life pattern. He continues expanding, and his view becomes bigger and wider and deeper as the years pass.

Hamada:

The simplicity of raku causes it to be the most difficult of all to make. The reason is that the usage of raku ware by the Japanese is very subtle. It is so simple that you must go through the full cycle of your development. I see it in terms of the four seasons. The best bowls are made by children who are unself-conscious. But just as you are reaching the peak of skill—summer—this is when the danger sets in. You become aware of your skill, and then you must get beyond that awareness before you can reach autumn and then winter. Then you must come into the next spring, not end with winter but arise with the next spring when the new buds form—the second spring. This is the period Japanese handcraftsmen know to be the time to develop their true craft. It is the second apple we are talking about, that is why it must be born, not made. Very often the craftsman does not live long enough, and not only that, when he is so old he may become brittle, rather than have a second childhood. If he becomes brittle, he must be very cautious. The second childhood must be a supple one, not a brittle one. To be able to make good red or black raku in Japan is the height of good potting because of this difficulty.

I have said for many years that I would try my hand at raku when I reached the age of seventy, but I have not done much yet. Because the low temperature firing keeps the form intact, with no firing distortion, I have been afraid that it would be essential for me to throw every pot with greater freedom and sensitivity. This made me hesitate. I think I shall make red and black raku when I do not feel they are difficult. Fortunately, a few years ago at an exhibition I was surprised to see a wonderful raku bowl covered with one simple buff-coloured glaze. I thought it should be regarded simply as pottery with a low-temperature glaze. And I decided to forget about the word raku and to think of it just as soft ware. I felt relieved.

No craft is easy to master. Pottery is among the most difficult to encompass. The reason may be that the glazing technique (which should be more properly called *yūgi*, play or pastime) and the firing technique are over-stressed. We should put aside this over-emphasis. The right way lies in plainness and naturalness. If we reflect on our motive for making pottery we can make a start without mistakes. I think we can approach the way of pottery much more easily then.

Leach:

When Hamada discussed his own work in 1973, he said that he did not know how to describe his own state now. He is not aware of his own state of being, but somehow he says that his work is indicative of how he is getting along. He can see that, without his knowing it, the pots show progress. It is a very strange thing—he is so busy and pressed in daily life; he is kept so busy doing all sorts of things, with so many visitors he has no time to do any quiet thinking. And yet his body knows what to do, and it is his body that goes ahead and does what is demanded of it. The result is quite satisfying. He would not say that everything comes out completely satisfactorily, but many of the pots do. He knows the truth of this, and he is very happy.

ALBUM

St. Ives, about 1900

*Shōji Hamada and our kiln, 1923
(suit by Ethel Mairet)*

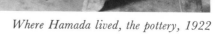

Hamada's firewood bed, the pottery, 1922

Where Hamada lived, the pottery, 1922

Hamada, my family, before our house, 1923

Old Basset with lobster, at the pottery, 1922

George Dunn

Matsubayashi and Hamada, St. Ives, 1923

Mrs. and Mr. Nance, Mrs. and Mr. Skinner, Hamada, self, walking in Cornwall, 1922

Mr. Pascoe, Hamada, self, son David, learning handle pulling at the Truro pottery, 1923

Matsubayashi, Mr. Mairet, Mr. Skinner, Hamada, Mrs. Skinner, Mrs. Ethel Mairet, Mrs. Mairet's mother, 1923

Henry Bergen, St. Ives, 1922

Staite Murray and Matsubayashi, Murray's oil kiln, 1923

Kazue Hamada just after marriage, arranging flowers in Truro pitcher, Mashiko, 1925

Hamada, Yanagi, self, St. Ives, 1929

Self, Yanagi, Hamada, Henry Bergen, Norah Braden, Michael Cardew, Katherine Pleydell-Bouverie's mother and sister, Coleshill, 1929

Hamada's main house just after reconstruction, Mashiko, about 1930

Reconstructing the large upper house, Mashiko, 1940s

Hamada showing slipware trailing to first son, Ryūji, Mashiko, about 1930

*Hamada, Yanagi, the painter Ryūzaburō Umehara, novelist Saneatsu
Mushanokōji, Tomimoto, Leach exhibition, Tokyo, 1933*

Hamada exhibition, Mitsukoshi department store, 1930s

Hamada in Mashiko, 1930s

*Hamada, Yanagi, Kawai, and self looking at a catfish,
Mashiko, 1934*

*Yanagi, self, Hamada, Kawai (r. of pillar), and friends, Naeshiro-
gawa, Kyushu, 1934*

Opening of first joint kiln at Hamada's, Mashiko, 1934

Hamada exhibition,
The Little Gallery, London, 1935

Hamada posing before a "likeness" on a wall in
Okinawa, 1930s

Weaver Yoshitaka Yanagi, textile artist Keisuke
Serizawa, Hamada, Yanagi, Kawai, Shiko Muna-
kata (?), others unidentified, in Kyushu, 1930s

Kazue Hamada, 1956

Hamada is nourished by honest work

Room of main house, Mashiko, 1950s

Youngest son, Yoshio, and English watches, 1950s

Masu Minagawa in her middle eighties, 1950s

Paddle-patterning a large jar

Hamada's workshop, 1950s

Same trio, Los Angeles, 1952

Yanagi, self, Hamada, Dartington Hall,
Devonshire, 1952

The three of us, Black Mountain College,
North Carolina, 1952

Maria Martinez and us, San Ildefonso, New Mexico, 1952

Working at Mashiko, 1953

Breakfast activity, Matsumoto, Nagano Pref., 1953

Yanagi, Kawai, self, Hamada, Chiba Pref., 1953

Gate-house

Main house

Upper gate-house

Large upper house (now containing craft collection)

Workshop

Aerial view of Hamada's compound

The small kiln

Paddling bottles

Hakeme

Decorating

Kiln opening

A toast, main room of Hamada's house

Hamada and Mrs. Hamada, Mashiko, 1960s

Grandfather

Kazue Hamada changing shoji paper, Mashiko, 1960s

Janet, self, Hamada, 1960s

Toyotarō Tanaka, Hamada, Sōichirō Ōhara (Ōhara Museum director) in Okinawa, 1960s

Hamada and son Shinsaku with us in St..Ives, 1963

Inside the collection house

Eames chair and Hamada on veranda of collection house

Painter Ryūzaburō Umehara, novelist Naoya Shiga, and Hamada at the Japan Folkcraft Museum, Tokyo, 1960s

Antique lacquer bowls, at the lacquer-ware town of Wajima, 1973

Self, feet, and Hamada, 1969

Tomimoto, Hamada, self, Kawai, Serizawa, dinner party, 1961

Tomimoto, Kawai, self, Hamada, symposium at Kurashiki, 1961

Hamada's craft museum, 1975

Three medieval English pots

PLATES

1. Bottle, hakeme. Okinawa.   h. 27.7 cm.   1927

2. Faceted bottle, cobalt, salt glaze.   h. 26.8 cm.   1959

3. Bottle, paddle pattern, iron pigment under nuka.   h. 30.7 cm.   1944

4. Faceted bottle, slip, enamels. Okinawa.   h. 24.2 cm.   1968

5. Square bottle, press-moulded, yellow ochre, iron pigment under nuka.　h. 28.6 cm.　1942

6. Bottle, paddled, nuka under tenmoku.   h. 30.0 cm.   1973

7. Bottle, paddled, iron pigment over transparent glaze. h. 23.0 cm. 1943

8. Bottle, paddled, white slip pours, manganese, cobalt, salt glaze.   h. 21.1 cm.   1968

9. Bottle, slip, underglaze iron and cobalt. Okinawa.   h. 28.2 cm.   1940

10. Rectangular bottle, press-moulded, tenmoku trailing over nuka.   h. 22.4 cm.   1966

11. Jar, underglaze iron.   h. 21.1 cm.   1926

12. Lugged jar, paddle pattern, yellow ochre, tenmoku under nuka.   h. 34.5 cm.   1948

13. Eared jar, nuka pours and iron pigments over nuka.   h. 17.9 cm.   1957

14. Bowl, transparent glaze, iron pigments.   h. 12.4 cm.   1953

15. Spherical lidded bowl, yellow ochre, iron pigment under nuka.   h. 18.2 cm.   1943

16. Large dish, kaki trailing over tenmoku.   d. 53.6 cm.   1962

17. Large dish, tenmoku trailing over nuka.   d. 56.2 cm.   1963

18. Plate, kaki trailing over tenmoku.   d. 26.8 cm.   1961

19. Square dish, press-moulded, iron pigment under nuka.   w. 19.8 cm.   1962

20. Square dish, press-moulded, wax resist, kaki.   w. 19.8 cm.   1962

21. Square dish, ash glaze over transparent glaze, enamels.   w. 19.8 cm.   1948

22. Bowl, slip, sgraffito, overglaze red enamel, cobalt, and iron. Okinawa.   d. 20.0 cm.   1967

23. Faceted brush-stand, slip, enamels. Okinawa.   h. 10.9 cm.   1968

24. Tea-pot, tenmoku with finger wipes.   h. 23.6 cm.   1941

25. Footed tea-pot, slip, enamels. Okinawa.   h. 18.5 cm.   1968

26. Yunomi, yellow ochre, overglaze iron pigments. h. 8.9 cm. 1953

27. Teabowl, incised, iron, salt glaze.   h. 10.2 cm.   1965

28. Teabowl, iron pigment over transparent glaze. h. 10.5 cm. 1934

29. Teabowl, cord-marked, incised, ash glaze.   h. 10.8 cm.   1949

30. Teabowl, combed, nuka and tenmoku over transparent glaze. h. 8.2 cm. 1952

31. Teabowl, nuka, tenmoku lip.   h. 7.8 cm.   1955

32. Teabowl, hakeme, iron pigments.   h. 10.0 cm.   1941

33. Teabowl, iron wash, transparent glaze, iron on lip.   h. 15.8 cm.   1937–38

34. Teabowl, hakeme, iron pigments.   h. 8.8 cm.   1943

35. Teabowl, ame glaze. h. 8.4 cm. 1955–60

36. Teabowl, tenmoku over nuka. h. 9.5 cm. 1947

37. Teabowl, iron pigments over transparent glaze.   h. 8.5 cm.   1971

38. Teabowl, slip, underglaze cobalt and iron, enamels.   h. 9.4 cm.   1972

39. Teabowl, iron wash under transparent glaze.   h. 8.6 cm.   1937

40. Teabowl, incised, manganese and cobalt, salt glaze.   h. 8.8 cm.   1971

41. Bottle, transparent glaze, wax resist, thin iron slip, iron pigment.   h. 35.9 cm.   ca. 1930

42. Bottle, impressed and paddle patterns, ame glaze.   h. 30.9 cm.   1953

43. Bottle, paddle pattern, ame glaze.   h. 19.0 cm.   1951

44. Square bottle, press-moulded, kaki trailing over tenmoku.   h. 28.5 cm.   1939

45. Square bottle, press-moulded, wax resist, kaki.   h. 23.8 cm.   1955

46. Saké bottle, overglaze ame and pigment. h. 13.6 cm. 1937

47. Jar, iron pigment under and over nuka.   h. 17.8 cm.   1943

48. Jar, press-moulded, tenmoku overlapping nuka.   h. 25.6 cm.   1960

49. Jar, white slip, transparent and black glaze pours. Okinawa.   h. 16.4 cm.   1940

50. Faceted brush-stand, copper green glaze over kaki.   h. 13.2 cm.   1941

51. Water-dropper, semi-porcelain, cobalt, iron pigment, enamels. h. 6.3 cm. 1943
52. Water-dropper, red, green, yellow enamels. h. 6.3 cm. 1940

53. Bowl, combed, cobalt, salt glaze.   h. 7.4 cm.   1958

54. Spouted bowl, tenmoku pours over nuka. h. 11.2 cm. 1943

55. Bowl, semi-porcelain, red and green enamels.   h. 10.0 cm.   1941

56. Bowl, incised, ash glaze.   h. 10.2 cm.   1952

57. Saké cup, semi-porcelain, cobalt and red enamel.   h. 3.5 cm.   1941
58. Saké cup, tenmoku pours over nuka.   h. 4.4 cm.   1946

59. Square dish, press-moulded, paddle pattern, tenmoku and nuka.   w. 29.3 cm.   1946

60. Large rectangular dish, copper green trailing over kaki. l. 44.0 cm. 1954

61. Rectangular dish, iron pigment patterns, wax resist, iron pigment. l. 22.0 cm. 1939

62. Incense box, semi-porcelain, underglaze cobalt, red and green enamels.   h. 5.2 cm.   1935
63. Incense box, iron and thin copper green.   h. 4.0 cm.   1937

64. Water-dropper, semi-porcelain, red and green enamels. h. 2.9 cm. 1941
65. Incense box, thrown and paddled, wax resist and kaki. h. 5.0 cm. 1937

66. Box, press-moulded, wax resist, iron pigment.   h. 11.1 cm.   1939

67. Box, press-moulded, iron pigments under nuka.   h. 12.8 cm.   1939

68. Incense box, slip, overglaze red enamel, cobalt, and iron. Okinawa.   h. 7.3 cm.   1940

69. Incense box, slip, chatter marks, overglaze iron and cobalt. Okinawa.   h. 7.1 cm.   1940

70. Incense box, semi-porcelain, red and green enamels. h. 8.7 cm. 1941
71. Incense box, slip, chatter marks, red and green enamel. Okinawa. h. 5.8 cm. 1940

72. Lidded pot, iron pigments over transparent glaze.   h. 9.5 cm.   1942

73. Faceted box, temmoku.   h. 12.3 cm.   ca. 1930

74. Incense box, wax resist, yellow ochre, thin ame glaze. h. 5.9 cm. 1931
75. Small lidded jar, slip, sgraffito, overglaze cobalt and iron. Okinawa. h. 6.5 cm. 1927

76. Tea-pot, transparent glaze, iron wash.   h. 15.5 cm.   1937

77. Small tea-pot, slip, underglaze iron and cobalt. Okinawa.   h. 14.3 cm.   1940

78. Small tea-pot, incised, wax resist, kaki.   h. 15.3 cm.   1942

79. Yunomi, slip, sgraffito, underglaze iron and cobalt. Okinawa.   h. 8.3 cm.   1940
80. Yunomi, tenmoku and ame over transparent glaze.   h. 8.5 cm.   1942

81. Teabowl, ame with finger-wipes.   h. 9.8 cm.   1939

82. Teabowl, combed, cobalt, salt glaze.   h. 9.1 cm.   1958

83. Teabowl, combed, manganese and cobalt, salt glaze.   h. 9.7 cm.   1968

84. Teabowl, wax resist, yellow ochre, tenmoku under nuka.   h. 10.4 cm.   1944

85. Teabowl, white slip pours, salt glaze. h. 9.7 cm. 1961

86. Teabowl, wax resist, yellow ochre, underglaze iron.   h. 8.3 cm.   1955

87. Teabowl, iron pigments over nuka. h. 8.2 cm. 1936

88. Teabowl, cord-marked, incised, ash glaze.   h. 8.8 cm.   1948

SKETCHBOOK

[The sketches included here and throughout the book are an edited selection from the sketchbooks in which Mr. Hamada has recorded and "eaten" craft objects and motifs. The facing page reproduces sketches by the author.—ed.]

facing page: left, pen sketches of Hamada pots, 1920s; Hamada's kiln, 1934; Hamada and a sequoia, 1952; right, Hamada, 1920; Hamada and chairs, 1934; Masu Minagawa and Mashiko tea-pot designs she drew in 1953, aged 81.

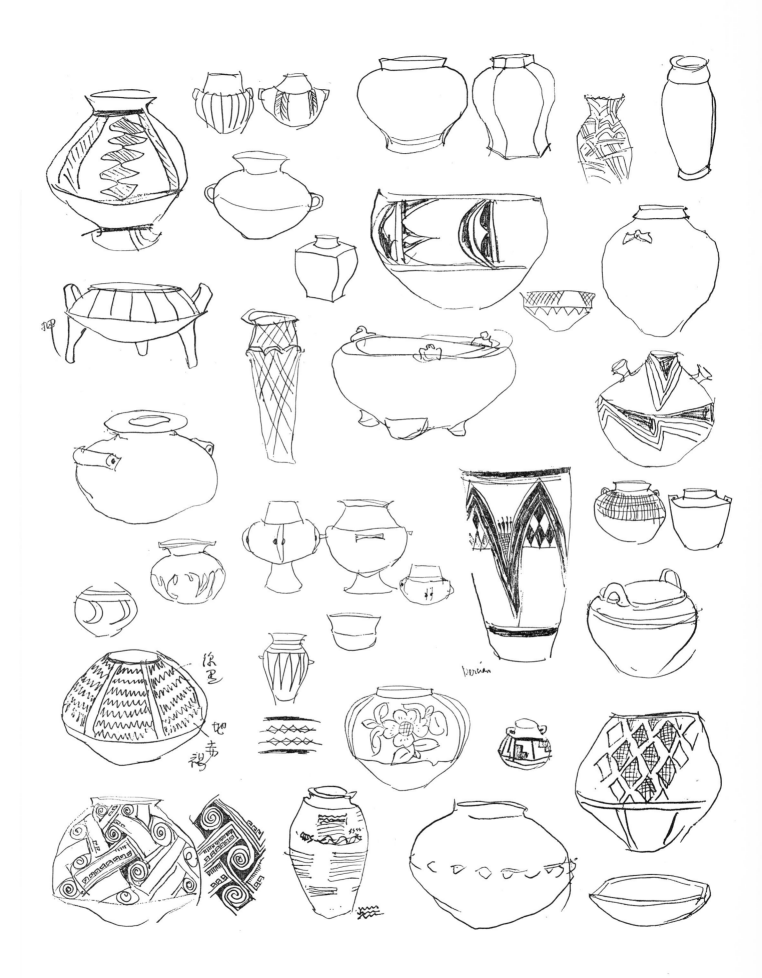

Byzantine Red fired vase

Beirut

Colombia

Bharleigh.

3000 B.C.

Mimbres (印)

鉢の陰

From the Island of Jersey.
water front
1800

六尺

我 幼 靜
臨 明 郡

中 寺

French

Comments on the Plates

[As the book was nearing completion, Mr. Hamada reviewed the plate captions. His comments, including some data supplementing the captions, are included here.—ed.]

1.   Hakeme is done directly on greenware in Okinawa. Hakeme slip will develop tiny pockmarks if applied just when the clay becomes white-dry, and sometimes cracks appear in the slip as well. Working directly on greenware is quite difficult; with Mashiko clay this is easier, but the Okinawan clay is very delicate.

Glaze can be applied when the slip has dried, but it adheres most evenly if applied when the slip is still wet. If this is done, the final effect will be quiet. Slip is applied when the clay is quite wet. With hakeme pieces I apply slip inside the piece while it is yet too wet to be able to turn the footring, and I even glaze the inside before turning. In any case, it is best to work as quickly as possible.

Glaze is applied to the inside twice. The first glaze coat is applied while the piece is glistening wet. The second coat goes on about twenty minutes (or one hour drying in the shade) after the first. Black glaze also may be used inside, but the lip and the areas where the inner neck is visible should be white like the outside.

The usual order of applying glaze is first the inside, then the outside, then again the inside. But with this hakeme piece, both inside glazings were finished before slip was applied to the outside. Therefore, this work must be fast. If you work on the outside first, it is too late to do the inside.

Of course, the hakeme slip was applied before glazing the outside.

Q.   Did you use a round brush?

A.   No, a flat one. But a large round brush is also possible.

Q.   Did you revolve the piece on a wheel to get the hakeme effect?

A.   When making many pieces, I simply revolve the piece on the wheel and do the hakeme in one smooth stroke, but with a few pieces and with larger ones, I use the brush with even strokes from both directions—from the right and the left. This change results in an interesting hakeme pattern. However, to begin with, hakeme was not meant to be appreciated for its brush texture, but was simply a means to apply a white slip to a dark clay body and make the slip adhere. Hakeme does not always come out as one hopes. It is not easy.

What is best for a particular pot must come out of the potter himself. If people start liking hakeme, they may want to use it for everything. The appropriate technique to be used for any pot has to emerge from the potter or the result is forced. I haven't been describing a set recipe for hakeme: each pot, each instance, makes its own demands to which there is an appropriate response. If you understand—digest and absorb—what hakeme was originally meant for and its effect, then you are free in using the technique. There is no absolute rule for hakeme. The best hakeme is quiet and yet appropriately dynamic.

2. thickly thrown and faceted. This piece is massive yet delicate and is quite effective when used for flower arrangements. Though I make many of these bottles, there are few with as much life as this one. Cutting the facets with a knife is very difficult, and a shape may loose its vitality in this process.

3. thrown and patterned; light and dark iron pigments, nuka glaze
   The pot is thrown up to the shoulder, then the incised paddle is used to pattern the piece. If there is no support on the inside, the paddle will push the clay in too far, so I put my hand inside to reinforce the clay behind the spot where I am applying the paddle. The piece is then left to dry a bit, after which the shoulder is constricted and the throwing finished. This type of paddled piece is also quite nice finished just with a coating of slip.

4. There is no biscuit firing in Okinawan pottery. Slip, transparent glaze, and enamels are applied, then the piece is fired.

5. wax resist (white areas), thin yellow ochre slip, biscuit firing, light and dark iron pigments, nuka glaze all over
   I have adjusted the glaze to make it thick and rich. This may cause what appear to be cracks or imperfections in the glaze, but it is best to be bold and to try such techniques. The results will be good.
   Q. Which is drawn first, the circles or the designs?
   A. The designs, then the circles. But either order is satisfactory.

6. This bottle was paddled on four sides, the corners bevelled, then the foot turned.
   Yellow ochre slip was applied, then the piece was biscuit fired; kaki glaze was applied inside first; nuka glaze was then applied on the outside; finally, it was dipped in tenmoku. One variation is to dip a piece in nuka, so that the nuka covers the upper two-thirds or so of the piece, and then to dip it in tenmoku from the bottom up until the tenmoku overlaps the nuka. With this technique, you get black on the bottom, a tenmoku and nuka combination in the middle, and pure white nuka on top [see Pl. 48].

7. After throwing this piece, I waited until it had hardened somewhat before paddling both flat sides and then, slightly, the narrower ends. Even with very little strength, the result of paddling can be clearly seen.
   Here the line is very soft, but this is a bold form. Someone asked for something formal, and this pot was considered the champion.
   yellow ochre, biscuit firing, transparent glaze, iron pigment.
   Pigment applied over the glaze results in mottling and colour variations and more life. Otherwise, you get a flat, enveloping effect; you invariably loose to the glaze. But your use of pigment over or under the glaze depends on whether you want to include a design. When pigment is applied under the glaze, you can adjust the effect by controlling the

glaze thickness; but when you use overglaze pigment, no compromise or afterthoughts are possible.

For the best results, this kind of work must be done quickly because the glaze immediately absorbs the iron pigment, which demands fast brush-work.

8. This piece is lightly paddled into an oval shape.
Q. Has the slip been applied with a ladle?
A. Yes. There is a real knack to using the ladle. You cannot be complacent even in using, for example, the various ordinary Mashiko brushes. Tools are things that cannot be taken for granted.

9. The cobalt and iron pigments are under the glaze in this piece, but may be applied either under or over the glaze.

10. This press-moulded bottle is made with a body mould that separates into two parts on the diagonal of the body; the foot and neck each have their own moulds.

The corners must be reinforced, and so the hand must be able to get inside the wet piece before the foot is applied. The corners are reinforced with clay, not slip.

First yellow ochre slip is applied and the piece is biscuit fired; nuka is applied, and then tenmoku is trailed over the nuka with a ladle. The two glazes—tenmoku and the nuka—run and shrink in the firing, exposing the ochre ground between the black and white.

The black pour must be done before the very thick application of nuka dries. This is a very simple technique.

11. This is a very early piece, and the technique is that of orthodox underglaze iron. I did not realize it at the time, but there appears to be a Yi dynasty iron pattern influence. But I did not want to copy the Yi pattern, and it has been many years now since I have done such work.

The technique is simple underglaze iron. A little later I started overglaze iron.

13. Yellow ochre is applied all over, the piece is biscuit fired, and nuka applied. A strong white nuka glaze is used for the ladle pour, and iron pigment and ame brush-work are applied.

15. wax resist stripes, yellow ochre, slip biscuit firing, iron pigment stripes, nuka glaze all over.

During the war, such pieces were made as containers for cooked rice.

It is usually said that the shape of pots and their potters are similar. Quite right—my pots usually come out roundish, even if I don't intend them to.

16. The contrast of the red and the black glazes is severe and appears hard. But the trailed glaze came out of the kiln just as I did it, without change. The orangish kaki colour is the result of reduction. The free effect of ladle trailing has made this technique popular, but it is not easy.

17. yellow ochre slip, biscuit firing, very thick nuka glaze, and freely applied tenmoku pours.

19. yellow ochre slip, biscuit firing, iron pigment, nuka glaze

20. biscuit firing, transparent glaze, wax resist design, kaki glaze all over. The black here is not the result of yellow ochre slip underneath.

People who don't understand what this glaze is enjoy this effect because the contrast is so clear. But those who do understand will think the effect strange.

21. biscuit fired, transparent glaze, wax resist, ash glaze, enamels. The harmony of this piece is very good.

22. The red enamel here has fired brown. Everyone says that this quiet colour is better for this piece than bright red enamel.

23. The red and green in this colour reproduction are too strong, but printers like the clearness of the brush-strokes and so these enamel pieces are always printed too colourfully.
Q. Is there iron pigment on the lip?
A. No. But because Okinawan slip flakes off sharp edges, I bevelled the lip to avoid this and then applied some manganese.
Q. Did you use wax here?
A. No. Where I put the green enamel over the red, mysteriously, the green erased the red underneath.

Because of the problem of Okinawan slip flaking off sharp edges, I also had to smooth the edges of the cut facets.

24. yellow ochre slip, biscuit firing, tenmoku, finger wipes.

25. My own ideas about form are included in this pot, but I also took advantage of the typical Okinawan forms for the feet and handle.

26. rough clay. I thought this clay was appropriate for teabowls, but I wanted to make something unusual. I first put on the vertical yellow ochre slip stripes, then the iron pigment brush-strokes.

The bottom of this yunomi is left rough, and this will become naturally and pleasantly discoloured with use. This technique is usually not used for yunomi, but for teabowls.

The glaze is transparent with some clay added.

28. yellow ochre slip inside, transparent glaze, iron pigment outside.

29. This is a very subdued piece. I rolled rope over the clay, but the cord-marked pattern was not clearly defined, so I bordered it with incised lines.

30. combing; transparent glaze all over, nuka glaze inside and on lip, tenmoku glaze on bottom. I inadvertently rubbed away some of the tenmoku, thus producing the kaki area on the left, which became the point of focus on the bowl.

31. yellow ochre slip outside only. The tenmoku on the lip was added to separate the rough outside from the smooth inside.

33. Same technique as that used in Plate 39, with the exception of the strong iron pigment added to the lip. If a solid colour comes out with such subtlety in variation, it is successful.

35. I did not intend it, but the turning tool took a deep bite into the clay and made a ridge that looks like an uphill slope. Another blessing is the effect of the slightly warped lip. All such features are gifts.

36. yellow ochre slip all over, nuka glaze all over, tenmoku glaze dip on lip and base

The ridge in the centre and the narrowed waist are of great help to old people, who no longer have much moisture in their hands. These features allow them to hold the bowl without its slipping through their fingers.

This piece has a warm feeling. The form is not found in so-called teabowls. I compromised by taking the conventional teabowl form and modifying it into my own version. I am happy with the result. I don't mean to denigrate ordinary teabowls—they are very fine. I do not want to make the mistake of walking the path of making teabowls by being negative about the conventional ones. I'd rather go firmly ahead and walk my own path.

37. Here I am being energetic. The bottom two-thirds of the bowl was left rough textured and will discolour nicely with use. On the pattern at the left I used light iron pigment for the horizontal and dark iron pigment for the vertical brush-strokes. It is only a little thing, but I reversed this order in the right-hand pattern. Even such things are now a matter of habit with me—I do not have to deliberate.

38. This is unabashedly bright and colourful, but it is a colourfulness that is not conscious of itself as being colourful. The red is where the red is, green is where green is, and they are made to dance together.

I have made many enamel pieces, but there is none in which the brush danced as in this one. Here the brush has not been overpowered by the colour, which is something that often happens. From that point of view, this piece is successful.

39. thin iron pigment (bottom-half only), transparent glaze; sandy body; bottom-half left rough textured

Q. Is this ash glaze?

A. No. It is transparent glaze with a large amount of clay.

This effect is close to that of the Korean Ido teabowls. The iron pigment is iron oxide with a little clay.

41. The iron here is pigment mixed with clay: one part iron and two parts clay. I adjust this formula according to the piece—for example, I use half and half, or reverse the proportions, using more iron than clay. The darkness of the pigment and its viscosity can thus be adjusted. The use of the brush is yet another way of adjusting the thickness and effect of the pigment. Variation in effect is desirable.

Sometimes I put iron pigment on iron pigment. Here, transparent glaze goes on first, after the biscuit firing, then wax resist, and then a pigment application, which may be either thick or thin. In making this piece, I applied a coat of dark pigment over the first coating and used a wheel to turn the pot under the brush. At times I may apply a freely brushed second coating. The point is not to be purposeful but to be natural.

Sometimes I start with a thin coat of pigment and then apply a thick coat to even it out, and sometimes the reverse, depending on what seems appropriate. It is not necessary to be concerned with achieving regularity or irregularity; the effort of the potter to achieve a specific effect will weaken the piece. If you are not worried about the pigment being even or uneven, the effect will certainly be good.

42. Here the pattern has been impressed with small moulds made of plaster or bis-cuitfired clay. A biscuited-clay mould is easier to use than a plaster one and makes a stronger impression.

This piece, just as with the pot in Plate 3, first was thrown only to the shoulder so I could put my hand inside to back up the clay when impressing the pattern.

Impressing leaves slight unevennesses on the pot's surface, which create pleasant effects when slip or glaze is applied. The accidents that occur as part of the use of materials and tools allow interesting results.

43. Here the paddling was done while the piece was still quite wet. The real trick is to start when the clay is not too wet nor too dry. If it is too wet, the pattern comes through clearly, but the paddling indents the body walls; if too hard, the body cracks.

The shoulders here are too rigid and angular. If I were to make this pot today, I would relax the shoulders more.

44. yellow ochre slip, tenmoku and kaki glazes

The kaki glaze was trailed with a rubber syringe, but this is not the most preferable tool because your fingers tire in squeezing it. A bamboo tube is much easier to use.

45. transparent glaze, wax resist, kaki glaze

46. transparent glaze, iron pigment, ame glaze

47. The round body shape of this vase can be seen anywhere, but what to do with the neck and lip? I solved the problem by making a round neck for the round body.

yellow ochre slip, biscuit fired, iron pigment, nuka glaze, iron pigment on neck and at bottom

If the ochre slip is too viscous, it should be thinned because it may peel off when it dries. On the other hand, if it is too thin, the colour will be weak. Mashiko people always laugh at me because I apply everything—slip, glaze, pigment—so generously. This is where I am different. The Mashiko people are very thrifty and are happy if the colour just comes through. Their black never comes out a true black.

48. Q. In a magazine I saw a reproduction of a small, brown, Chinese jade object dated to the Warring States period; its shape was very similar to that of this piece. But the magazine photo was enlarged to almost full-page size.
A. Yes, I have seen such a jade piece, and it was quite small.

Enlarging something is an act of interpretation in itself, and an object is transformed by the person who enlarges it. What it is that makes someone stop enlarging something at the point that feels right—that is the act of interpretation. Mechanical magnification is easy, but it takes someone to decide to stop at the right place.

It is through the understanding—the eyes—of the observer that the thing itself is transformed and given a new life. To imbue something with attributes—to see an object as being good, bad, or whatever—makes that object no longer what it really is. Should I make something this way or that way; how should I twist it or shape it—such *thoughts* are all extraneous. Even if you don't have such thoughts, just to think something is good makes that something what it isn't. It is in this direction of no categories that one comes to grips with one's work. But usually if you admire something, you become attached to it and can't break away, and your work becomes progressively worse.

The technique used for this piece is the same as that described in Plate 3 except that the nuka glaze has not been applied to the entire pot. If the nuka glaze is too white, a severe effect is produced, so I first applied ochre slip all over.

I leave it to the kiln to provide the subtleties. Even if the kiln is asked by me to do its work, if that kiln is fired by somebody else, it can't do the same kind of work as when I do the firing.

If I think I am imitating something, and if it is successful, it is not at all an imitation. This is a distinction that most people cannot make, and their footing is unsure.

49. No biscuit firing in Okinawa; glazed when very soft.
     white slip, transparent and black glaze pours

50. rough body; surface left rough on top and bottom; transparent glaze, kaki glaze, copper-green glaze brush-marks

51. biscuit fired, underglaze cobalt, transparent glaze, wax resist, iron pigment, red and green enamels

54. yellow ochre slip, biscuit fired, nuka glaze inside, tenmoku glaze ladle pours

55. I have tried about thirty patterns with overglaze enamels, of which about one-half I think are successful.

57. small red enamel dots at tips of cobalt lines

58. yellow ochre slip, nuka glaze, tenmoku ladle pours
Q.   When I first saw a photo of this piece, I thought it was much bigger. The proportions are those a large piece would have. Have you any thoughts about keeping the same proportions of form and design regardless of the size of the piece?
A.   Thought does not enter here. The eyes and body do all the commanding—how and how much. The problem doesn't even reach "headquarters."

59. When this was still in the press mould, I paddled the pattern. The tenmoku glaze is ladled on first, then the nuka glaze edge. I never get tired of this shape and am still making these dishes now.

60. This pot is actually luted slabs. The joints are points of weakness, and one must be extremely careful to press the joints firmly together and lute them.
     biscuit fired, transparent glaze, kaki applied immediately, ladled copper-green trailing, second coat of transparent glaze.
     This glazing is very carefully done.

61. Among the pieces I have made with this iron pigment, this piece turned out the best. The iron pigment design is painted first, then the compasses are used, then transparent glaze, wax resist, the ame glaze is added to the iron design, the iron pigment background is applied, and finally a second coat of transparent glaze.

63. biscuit-fired, transparent glaze, iron pigment and thin copper-green glaze

65. thrown and paddled; transparent glaze, wax resist, kaki glaze

66. transparent glaze, wax resist, iron pigment

67. white body; press-moulded; thin iron pigment stripes, transparent glaze mixed with some nuka glaze, ame glaze then brushed between iron pigment stripes [not clear on tape whether pigment is underglaze or overglaze]

Having worked with moulds this long, you would think that my moulds would improve, but this is not so. At a very early point I seem to have exhausted that which I could express in mould form. Though one may gradually modify moulds, such modifications are actually afterthoughts. The essence of the piece seems to have been expressed in the making of the first mould. A man is the same—one's capacity to express himself all comes out at an early stage. But you can't eat with this philosophy, so you carry on using the same mould for years and years.

68. slip, transparent glaze, iron pigment and cobalt, enamels

69. slip, chatter marks and incising, transparent glaze, iron pigment and cobalt

72. transparent glaze, iron pigment and ame glaze, thin iron pigment on lid top
The rough texture results from turning the piece while the clay is still quite wet.

76. This piece has discoloured and mellowed with daily use just like a teabowl. Yanagi used this tea-pot for years.

The bottom one-third was left rough. Transparent glaze, thin iron pigment applied to bottom. Same technique as for teabowl shown in Plate 39.

78. transparent glaze (?), incising, wax resist, kaki glaze

80. transparent glaze, ame glaze and tenmoku glaze lines alternating (the dot is accidental)

81. transparent glaze under ame glaze, finger wipes
While the glaze is still wet, I gently wipe the body with the sides of the fingers, hardly touching it. When Sakuma tried this technique, he used the tips of his fingers, and after a day his fingers hurt so that he could not work further.

85. white slip trailed with a ladle. If you give the pot a tap after applying a blob of slip, it will run like this.

86. This design is based on the pattern of American Indian baskets. Anybody can do this design. The angles of the lines, both black and white, have been filled in. This very simple touch is the same as the weave of the basket, but such wisdom does not come to one easily. I owe this idea to having seen the Indian baskets.

87. yellow ochre slip, nuka glaze, dark and light iron pigments

88. perhaps a paddle wrapped in a rough textile was used to texture this piece; thin ash glaze

Index

THE AUTHOR: Bernard Leach was born in Hong Kong in 1887. He attended art school in England and went to Japan in 1909 as an artist and etcher. His initial interest in pottery there soon developed into a total commitment, and in 1920 he returned with Shōji Hamada to England, where he founded the Leach Pottery in St. Ives, Cornwall.

Today Mr. Leach is undoubtedly the most famous potter in the Western world. As teacher, writer, philosopher, and artist, he has set up standards that have permeated the entire craft world. This book is the companion volume to *The Unknown Craftsman*, the author's English adaptation of Sōetsu Yanagi's aesthetics of craft and "born" work. The three friends—Leach, Hamada, and Yanagi—have forged a bond between East and West that will have a permanent effect on craft technique and philosophy.